YOU
WERE
BORN
TO
SPEAK

...SO WHAT'S HOLDING YOU BACK?

Get the results, reactions and respect you deserve
every time you speak

by
RICHARD NEWMAN

Editor: Judy Barratt

Designer: Dave Brown at Ape

Print production: Emma Dixon at Urban Print Support

Illustration: Ivana Zorn

Cataloguing in Publication Data: a catalogue record for this book is available from the British Library.

ISBN 978-1-9164592-0-5

Printed in England by CPI Colour

'Richard Newman is one of the most thoughtful and incredibly creative teachers of communication I've come across in my career.'

DAVID MURRAY

DIRECTOR OF PROFESSIONAL SPEECHWRITERS' ASSOCIATION, USA
AWARD-WINNING JOURNALIST, BESTSELLING AUTHOR

'The techniques Richard teaches are world class. He has electrified our team and helped to increase our results.'

AIT VONCKE

SENIOR VICE PRESIDENT, EXPEDIA

'These strategies transformed the way our team communicates, accelerating our progress and boosting our success. Richard and his team have a rare skill for teaching powerful techniques in a dynamic way and delivering real-world results.'

NICK BONNEY

FORMER HEAD OF INSIGHTS, CAMELOT AND EE

INSPIRE

CONNECT

MOTIVATE

PERSUADE

CAPTIVATE

COLLABORATE

Speak up, be heard and tilt the world
in a more positive direction.

DEDICATION

Max and Ted, my two amazing sons, I am writing this book for you. You have so much energy, brilliant imaginations and such passion for living. You were born to express yourselves, dream big ideas and bring them to life. My interactions with you have helped me to see how much extraordinary potential we all have to connect with each other. You are both fully present and captivating in every moment.

As you grow older you will face challenges, failures and situations that may diminish your confidence. When you share your ideas, people may ignore you, talk over you or reject you. As a result you may feel like building up your defences against people to protect yourselves.

I urge you to resist this feeling. Hold on to your connection with people. Those reactions and responses don't mean that your ideas are not worth listening to. You may simply need to adjust how you communicate, so that people care, understand and feel motivated by what you say.

This isn't easy to achieve, but it is a lot simpler when you remember that you were born to speak. This book was written to explain what this means and to help you live your dreams.

I hope to be with you every day, to walk by your side through all of life's challenges. However, one day, if I'm no longer here and you need help with an important event, I wanted to leave you with this book so that you can become all you can be, shine your light and share your voice.

YOUR SUPPORT MATTERS

The profits from this book will be shared with the following charities, so that more young people are given the support they need to fulfil their potential.

Afrikids

I have supported Afrikids for over a decade, through donations and coaching the charity's team to improve their impact. I know how brilliant and dedicated the Afrikids team is. The charity has transformed the lives of thousands of people in Ghana. Let's help it to continue its amazing mission to bring big smiles to little faces.

Pema Tsel Academy

When I was eighteen I went to live in a monastery in India, where I taught English to monks. The head monk, Paljor La, set up a school for children in a remote area of India, where they previously had no opportunity for an education. I am proud to help pay the teachers' salaries and maintenance of the buildings to give a brighter future to the children who attend and live at the school.

Room To Read

Room To Read invests in nearly one million children each year in low-income countries, by focusing on literacy and gender equality in education. Working with local communities and governments, they help primary-school children with reading and writing, as well as supporting girls to complete secondary school with the life skills they need to succeed. They aim to invest in the lives of 15 million children by 2020. We can help them get there.

Thank you for buying this book. Your contribution will help these charities give healthcare, safety and education to children.

Contents

FOREWORD

WHERE DID THE JOURNEY BEGIN?

Do you remember an experience that you would rather forget, a painful memory of a day when things went wrong? For me, it happened when I was seventeen. I was a shy kid and I had a terrible fear of public speaking. In fact, I was so bad at communicating that a year earlier, for my sixteenth birthday, a friend bought me a book on body language to help improve my people skills.

I was amazed by what I learned from reading that book. I felt I had been given the holy grail – a key to understanding people in a way that I never had before. I wondered, 'What's wrong with me? Why are other people more natural at these things? Why can't I connect with people in the same way?'

Then a fateful day arrived. I was a student at an all-boys school and two miles away there was an all-girls school. One day, the girls' school decided to invite the boys to come along for a public speaking competition. I couldn't resist the opportunity to go along to their school (I finally had the opportunity to sit in the company of women!), but there was no way I was going to take part.

I found a seat on the back row. I kept my coat on and hunkered down into it, praying that nobody would notice me.

The competition began. Volunteers stood at the front of the room to speak, I hid in safety and everything was going well. I even started to relax a bit. I remember thinking, 'I'm not that impressed with what the speakers are saying. If I had the confidence to get up there I think I'd have something worthwhile to say.' But, out of fear, I kept silent.

Once all the speakers had finished, the audience was invited to ask questions. A teacher leaned over to me. He tapped me on the shoulder and passed me a note with a question written on it. He said, 'Read this out loud to everyone.' My heart started beating so hard I could feel it pounding in my chest. I could sense all the blood draining from my face and my body froze.

I couldn't speak. I couldn't function. I found it difficult to breathe.

Finally the teacher gave up on me and passed the piece of paper to somebody else. I had been given one chance to make a good impression and I'd blown it.

I desperately wanted to avoid being in that situation again. I thought that some people were born to speak and some weren't. I clearly was not.

Just a few weeks later everything changed. One of my closest friends was a thoughtful, hard-working and incredibly intelligent young man, with a dream of going to Oxford University. While the rest of us spent the summer at the park, parties or the pub, he read books. Before Google existed, if you wanted to know something you just had to ask him.

He took the Oxford entrance exam and sailed through it. The university invited him for an interview and shortly afterwards we were all waiting for the day when we would celebrate him getting accepted. In fact, we got him a card and on the envelope we wrote, 'Oxford Oxford, you're our man, if you can't get in, no one can!!'

When I gave him the card he took one glance at the envelope and looked defeated. He simply said, 'I didn't get in.' I couldn't believe it.

He handed me a letter that had arrived that morning effectively telling him that he was clearly a very bright young man, but that he lacked the communication skills the university required to be able to offer him a place.

In that moment I knew two things. First, Oxford had missed out on having one of the brightest, kindest and most dedicated students it could ever wish for. Second, that I would never be as intelligent as him, so I had better get damn good at communicating, otherwise what chance did I have of ever achieving anything in my life?! I suddenly saw how important communication is to success, regardless of grades, character and knowledge.

Twenty years later, I found myself on stage in front of seven hundred people, teaching communication skills. I felt humbled by the audience, who gave four standing ovations in our three-hour workshop together. At the end, as they started to leave, one person came up to me and said, 'Wow, I wish I could do what you do, but I'm terrified of this stuff. You are clearly a natural.'

It felt so surprising and confusing to hear this. Inside I was still that shy schoolkid, hiding on the back row. Over the years I had simply learned how to access the instincts we are all born with to become the speaker I wanted to be. I reflected on the journey I had taken.

'Actually no,' I replied. 'I'm nothing special. I used to be terrified of doing this. All you need to do is follow certain principles and practise. You can do it too.' The woman looked back at me in disbelief. Could it be true? I began to tell her the things that I have now written in this book, in order to help her speak up, stand out and be heard.

I would love to share with you what I learned in the twenty years between those two events, so that you can fulfil your potential. Whether you need to talk in a meeting, or give a pitch or a speech, your ability to communicate, influence and inspire people is critical to your success. This book is designed to help you be confident and compelling whenever you speak, so that you can achieve your goals, make your ideas happen and gain the results and respect you deserve.

I'll start by introducing you to the foundations and science that will support you in reaching your true potential. Then, we'll look at three major areas on which great communicators rely:

- **Style**: transform your personal impact and increase your presence through using your body and voice more effectively, with activities to bring your behaviour back to its natural, authentic best

- **Story**: understand the way people are born to listen, so that you can turn your ideas into engaging stories that compel an audience to listen and are easy for them to remember. You'll learn how to apply this to a range of situations, from speaking on the spur of the moment in meetings, to writing an important pitch or speech

- **State**: learn to be your greatest self whenever you need to, overcoming challenges with techniques you can apply before and during important events, allowing you to enjoy your life and make ideas happen

Thankfully, all of this may be easier to master than you imagine, because you were born to do it.

Let me explain what this means and how this principle will help you to become the best communicator you can be.

For me, the adventure started with a trip to a monastery...

INTRODUCTION

YOU WERE

BORN TO DO IT

Chapter 1
You were born to connect

...but how do you communicate without words?

I'm in the wrong place, thousands of miles from home, drinking hot, salty butter, with people who don't speak English. How did this happen?

A couple of weeks after those painful experiences at school, I attended a talk given by one of our past students about gap years. At the start of his talk, he asked how many of us were considering taking time off before we started university to do something meaningful for a year. Three students – out of the 150 in the room – raised their hands. One of those hands was mine.

What? Hold on. This was not the plan. I had a place at university and that's where I was going. But something about this guy grabbed my attention. His face was familiar from the time he'd been at the school, but he looked wiser now, and more at peace.

He described his extraordinary experience. A charity had given him some training in how to teach communication skills overseas, and off he went. Before he knew it, he was travelling on the roof of a bus in Nepal to find an orphanage where he was to teach English to children. It sounded like the trip of a lifetime. I was hooked.

I contacted the charity and asked to go to the most remote place available, somewhere that I could really help people. They told me there was a Tibetan monastery in the foothills of the Indian Himalayas, where the monks wanted to learn English to help them connect with their community. That's perfect, I thought. I signed up.

Before my trip I took a one-week crash course in teaching English as a foreign language. The course involved mainly learning ice-breaker games to help students get to know one another and how to write words and phrases on a classroom whiteboard. Both techniques would prove to be completely useless when I discovered that the monks had known each other for years and had no classroom!

However, one thing we learned really stood out. Our tutor said that she would teach us how to speak Chinese by speaking to us only in Chinese. To my amazement in the space of five minutes I had learned ten Chinese words simply by watching and listening to her sounds and gestures.

A few days later I was on a plane to India, a wide-eyed, innocent teenager on his first overseas trip without his parents, hoping to make the world a better place. I landed in the heart of Delhi. If you've been to Delhi, you'll know it's a tough place to start any journey. You're hit with sensory overload: frantic traffic, endless noise and the self-consciousness of people staring at you (Indian friends have since told me that staring is their main national pastime, after cricket). I spent two days travelling by train, jeep and taxi to reach my destination – Kalimpong. By the time I got there, I had barely spoken to anyone and was keen to see the monks' friendly faces.

I took a taxi to the monastery, where the monks very kindly sat me down with a flask of Tibetan tea and looked thoughtfully at me. I explained who I was and what I was there for. They spoke softly in Tibetan among themselves before gesturing that I should drink the tea. I would grow to love the Tibetan people, but I never understood how they could drink this stuff. It's made with black tea, yak butter, and salt. I felt it would be rude not to finish my cup, so I drank the whole thing, trying not to gag, as they murmured to each other.

Sensing that they were confused, I showed them the letter I had been sent, inviting me to come to teach. They started gesturing. One seemed to be saying I should stay, the other pointed to the front door. Together we realised that the symbol on my letter did not match the one above their doorway. I was in the wrong monastery. This all seemed rather strange to me. I mean, how many Tibetan monasteries could there be in a small hill town in India? Nonetheless, I thanked them for the tea and left.

At the next monastery, I received much the same response. Tea, confusion, gesturing and realising that I was once again in the wrong place. This happened twice more. Each time I was greeted by Tibetan monks who welcomed me, gave me tea, then indicated I should leave. By this point I was determined that nobody should brew salty-yak-butter until I knew if I was staying or not!

At the fifth monastery, finally, above the entrance, I saw the symbol that matched my letter. Success! Beyond this door would be a group of monks happily awaiting me, ready to learn English.

Two of them came to greet me.

'It's so good to meet you,' I said. 'It was really difficult to find you, but it looks like I'm finally in the right place.'

They looked blankly at me, then at each other, then back at me. They didn't understand a word I was saying. Although I was in the right place, things were not quite as I expected. I thought I was there to improve their English. It turned out that most of the monks couldn't speak any English… at all.

I would soon learn that they could speak Tibetan, Nepali and Hindi. I knew only English (plus a bit of high-school French and German), so we didn't have a common language. The challenge I would face, while living with them for six months, was figuring out how to teach them anything without the use of words.

They led me to their kitchen and we sat down. We looked at each other silently for a while. Then I remembered the teacher who had taught me a few words of Chinese. I began to speak slowly, while gesturing, using my face and tone to indicate what I was saying. After some trial and error, I found out where I would sleep, eat and teach.

We held the classes in the kitchen, after sunset. There were electricity blackouts daily, usually during the evening, so I often taught by candlelight. I didn't have a mobile phone. There were no computers (and certainly no email or Internet). Social media didn't exist. If I posted a letter it took six weeks to arrive in the UK, meaning that the fastest reply I could get would take three months from the moment I sent my own letter. The monastery had a landline telephone that worked for about one hour a week. And even when I did get through, the voice on the other end sounded like a person yelling down a coal-mine during a lightning storm.

I felt cut off from the rest of the world and very far from home. However, the monks and I ventured forwards with our lessons. Each evening we would gather and I would attempt to teach them a few more words. A couple of months after I arrived, the monks could speak basic English. We moved on to more complex notions. I especially remember teaching them how to tell the time. I couldn't understand why they found the lesson so confusing, until I realised that they couldn't tell the time in any language, let alone in English! Later on I taught them prepositions, how to express emotion in what they were saying and more complex sentences.

After six months they could all have a reasonable conversation in English with me and I had learned to speak Nepali. In fact, I could speak Nepali far more fluently than I'd ever been able to speak French or German at school. Our success in learning so much from each other had happened thanks to non-verbal communication, congruency and getting back to basics.

Some people think that body language is surface-level nonsense, manipulation, or pretending to be something you're not. I discovered that there is much more to it than that. *For me, body language is the deeper way that we can all connect with each other, without the use of words, where we tap into something more natural and meaningful.*

In order to communicate more powerfully we need congruency between our words, body and voice. This is where great communication begins.

CONGRUENCY – WHERE DID IT ALL GO WRONG?

Modern life has stripped away congruency. Many people work in open-plan offices, where they have to mute their voices so that they don't distract others. Company cultures often focus on behaving 'professionally', which sometimes gets translated to mean 'impersonally'. Out of fear of showing how we really feel at work, we limit our expression. Congruency disappears, and it becomes much harder to understand what people really mean.

While working with the monks I had to be completely congruent every day, just to be understood. For example, if I was trying to teach them the word 'excited', but I didn't look excited or sound excited, then I might as well have been saying 'pineapple'. My physical and vocal communication had to match my meaning.

From monks to movie stars

After six months, I came back from India. I wanted to study communication in more depth, so I enrolled in a three-year course at a London acting school. Despite my concerns that I might be made to dress in tights or stand like a tree, I thought that acting skills would teach me how to really connect with an audience. In my first week, though, one of the teachers said, 'We will not be teaching you how to act.' Huh?!

'Instead,' she said, 'we will be helping you to remove the habits and behaviours that are holding you back, so that you are free to perform at your best.' Okay, I was in the right place!

It seemed bizarre to show up to an expensive course every day to be told how to sit, how to stand, how to walk, how to move and how to breathe. I was fairly certain that I could do all of these things perfectly well. However, when I watched the other students, it was clear what a difference small changes could make. People who had at first seemed rigid became more open, captivating and confident.

Another teacher told us, 'If you're an actor then your job is all about subtext. You can't change the words, but you can change what they mean and how people react to them.' In business the subtext of your message can be lost in emails, phone calls or poker-face meetings. I have been to many conferences where a speaker has opened with 'I'm delighted to be here today' while looking and sounding as though he were at a funeral.

This lack of congruency becomes worse when people stand behind a lectern. Can you imagine telling a young child that if they want to talk to you about something important they should stand behind a box? To make things worse, lecterns are usually positioned on the side of the room, away from the screen. Slides are filled with countless words, forcing the audience to read the presentation rather than connect with the speaker. These barriers may make a speaker feel safe, but communication is not about doing things that make you feel better. It is about giving other people what they need from you.

You need to give people the subtext, which is much easier when people can see your face and your body. Professional communication isn't about leaving your personality at the door. It's about using your voice to bring ideas to life and connecting with people. Much of the training I gained as an actor was about undoing the habit of hiding myself and bringing back congruency so that I brought to life the meaning in every message I wanted to convey.

I must admit that I struggled. I thought that if I could feel the way a character was supposed to feel, then the audience would feel it too. I soon discovered that the thoughts and feelings in my head weren't coming alive in my performance. As Jim Carrey once said, 'You are not who you think you are, you are only what you communicate.' While he is known for his exaggerated expressions (which is more than most of us ever need), like many great actors, he can change the way people feel. He called it 'the greatest currency there is'.

I shall always be grateful to one of our teachers, a Canadian movement coach called Ed, who showed us that shifting our posture and arms could influence the response of an entire audience. He called it 'non-verbal leakage'. We can leak information to an audience about how we feel without saying a word. And we don't need any silly manipulation devices. We can do it by stripping back the layers of habit that hide us away so that we can express ourselves authentically.

You may feel that you're already a fairly natural communicator. You may aim to be truthful. Neither of these traits necessarily makes you congruent. Habits get in the way without you even realising it. Throughout the book we'll explore ways to overcome them so that you can become the most authentic and engaging version of yourself.

Most people that I have worked with suffer a lack of congruency. Perhaps you know people who speak softly all the time. They will tell you 'I'm just a quiet person.' But people are not born softly spoken. At birth, no one pops out of the womb and whispers gently, 'I would really like some milk.' Instead, a baby's first noise is so loud, powerful and emotional, it compels as many people as possible to help. Speaking quietly isn't a natural behaviour. It is learned. But some people practise quiet speaking for so many years that when they want to speak up in a meeting, only a mere squeak comes out.

You may not suffer with a quiet voice yourself, but you are very likely to have other behaviours that limit your ability to communicate. These habits soon become so comfortable that they feel as though they are instinctive. So much so that they compel you to say things like, 'That's just who I am.' Breaking free from habitual patterns of behaviour and going back to how you were born to speak liberates you, restores congruency and enables you to connect much more easily with those around you. In turn, this allows you to transform how others feel about you and your ideas.

The damage of screen time

I spent much of my young life as a shy introvert. This means that I spent a lot of time learning about the world through television.

The amount of time you spend in front of screens has a detrimental impact on your communication skills. The negative effect starts from an early age. As John Medina explains in his book *Brain Rules for Babies*, young children cannot learn language effectively by watching television. They need to be with people.

Many companies that claimed to sell videos that would teach children how to speak have had to stop. An experiment that established how we actually learn language proved that such videos do not work. In the study two groups of young children were taught using two methods. The first group had a teacher actually sitting in front of them; the second were shown a video of the same teacher giving the same lesson. The first group learned a few words; the second group did not. Why?

Communication skills are essential for survival. To a child, a parent or guardian makes sounds that could be critical for safety.

Noises from a screen, however, don't have the same emotional effect – they don't feel as real or as important.

It's not just babies and children that need time away from screens. As adults we spend so much time in front of screens that the number of hours we have left for observing and interacting with other humans is much reduced, limiting the amount of experience we gain in how to express ourselves and connect with people. People of all ages need to spend time with each other to become skilled in the subtleties of congruent communication.

One screen that many agree has a terrible impact on communication is the presentation slide filled with bullet points. Bullet points rarely explain a message in a meaningful and memorable way. An audience stares at the slides (when not staring at a phone or laptop screen). But does any of the information actually go in if we're reading a list rather than connecting with the speaker?

Our earliest ancestors – long, long, long before any screen technology – needed to be great communicators for survival. If you gathered your tribe around a campfire with only one chance to tell them about your escape from the claws of a sabre-toothed tiger, your message needed to be not only clear, but compelling and memorable. Only then might your survival tactics save lives for the next hunting group, and so by extension your species. What if the only visual reminders of your survival were drawings on a cave wall? The most compelling information verbally and visually is conveyed in ways that tap into our primal instincts for survival. Not through bulleted lists.

Every day during my acting training we had to bring stories to life. No set, no costume, no slides, no handouts. We had to fully engage the people around us, so that they understood the story, the subtext and the intention, and so that they felt moved by the delivery.

By the end of the first year, I was ready to give in. I couldn't do it. I was being criticised by every teacher after every performance. I could see other people succeeding while I struggled to make any progress. Perhaps this was the end of the road, I thought. I wasn't a natural communicator and never would be.

MAYBE ONLY SOME PEOPLE ARE BORN TO SPEAK

I was contemplating giving up my acting studies when everything changed, thanks to a packet of cigarettes and a game of whispers.

It was the start of our second year and we were learning about props and presence. I had barely mastered how to remember my lines and not fall over the furniture! Now we were having to make tea, the old-fashioned way with a strainer and teapot, while reciting a speech. My brain couldn't function. I even poured a bottle of water over another actor, because I didn't realise he was miming holding a glass, rather than using a real one!

Then a breakthrough. I was doing a Noël Coward play, and my character was a suave smoker. I've never smoked and I had no idea how tricky it is to light a cigarette while holding a lighter in one hand and a packet of cigarettes in the other.

We were doing a run-through of the play, but we had to whisper every line as quietly as possible, so that the other actors could barely hear us. This meant that our listening skills became very acute and we had to work extra-hard to connect with each other. I had to do all that and light the cigarette. Then, the lighter stopped working.

My brain didn't have the capacity to worry about my performance, listen to the others and get the cigarette alight. All I could do was think about the lighter. I half started saying my line several times. When finally I got the cigarette alight, I sighed, turned to the other actors who were focussed intently on me and said my line with palpable (congruent!) relief.

It was the first time I remember getting a laugh as an actor and it was the point at which everything began to make sense. Year one at acting school was about stripping away bad habits. Now we were bare. Free to communicate. The whispering and prop malfunction meant that I and everyone on the stage was fully present. We were fully connected. We could collaborate. Just as we were born to.

Why are human beings the dominant species on the planet? We're not the fastest, nor the strongest. Many animals that were more physically powerful than us have long since become extinct. In the book *Sapiens: A Brief History of Humankind*, historian Yuval

Noah Harari explains that while we may want to believe that humans are special, a lone chimpanzee would have a much better chance at surviving on a desert island than a human. A lone human is not special. The human gift is the ability to collaborate in very large numbers by communicating empathetically, flexibly, adaptably and for the greater good.

Chimpanzees can work together, but only if they know each other personally and in groups of, at most, twenty. Bees can work in larger numbers, but they are not flexible or adaptable (it's the queen bee's way or the highway). Humans are instinctively flexible and adaptable enough to be able to work together in huge numbers. We can communicate collectively and collaboratively. As a result we can achieve great results (not least our species' survival) and work together in unity.

RECLAIMING YOUR INSTINCTS

This book is called *You Were Born to Speak* because I believe that the greatest barrier that many people face to good communication is thinking that they are not born able to communicate well. This is nonsense. Communication is essential for your survival and you have far greater instincts for it than you may realise. All you need to do is reawaken them.

A few years ago I was running a compulsory workshop about communication at work. Before we started I noticed a man in his late fifties, leaning back in his chair, frowning and saying, 'No, no, no!' to the person next to him. I went over to ask what they were discussing. He announced with great certainty, 'This workshop is pointless. You can either talk to people or you can't. You can't teach this stuff.'

Although it makes life easier if the people I teach have chosen to be there, I look forward to working with people who are told to attend, knowing that those who would never just sign up may gain the most.

With this in mind I asked the man why he felt this way. He told me that he had been on other training courses that had never achieved anything for him. He thought that this session would be just as useless.

In her book *Mindset*, Carol S. Dweck explains that if you have a fixed mindset, believing that you can either do something or not, you will achieve far less in all aspects of your life than if you are open to challenge. In fact, studies show that children who are praised for being smart may give up when they struggle with something new. They fear that failing a task may prove they are not smart after all.

Those with a 'growth mindset' are able to learn new skills and are much more likely to keep trying after failing. Children who are praised for working hard, rather than being told they are smart, are more likely to develop this mindset and will keep striving to achieve something when others give up.

This man appeared to have a fixed mindset. I needed to shift his thinking about how much he could achieve so that he could reach his true potential. I explained that I used to feel the same way as him. I had been through a struggle to rid myself of bad habits and fears. I had changed from a shy schoolboy who was terrified to speak up to a highly paid speaker. I wanted to help other people achieve the same.

His face shifted. He was still uncertain, but he was more open to the notion that someone could teach him to leave his habits behind and reap the rewards of good communication. His body relaxed, his expression softened and his mind opened. At the end of the workshop he thanked me for helping to awaken his instincts.

I encourage you also to keep an open mind about how much you can improve and achieve while reading this book. This is especially important if you feel that you are already a good communicator and are just looking for a couple of new tips. When you think 'I already know what I'm doing,' you may find it harder to drop your old habits and grow further. I encourage you to put your current strategies to one side as you keep reading.

If you feel uncomfortable trying out something you read in here, then it could be because it is 'messing with your armour'. I had this experience recently at a personal development conference. I felt vulnerable letting go of past behaviours that had helped me to cope with certain situations, but I couldn't make any progress until I did. It was essential to drop old habits in order to take my life to a new level.

Similarly, you may have strategies that you use to communicate that have given you some success, and you may fear that if you let them go, you'll stop succeeding. Notice if this happens and trust that you can let the armour go. After all, the path to greater success may be ahead of you. In fact, your armour may have been weighing you down and holding you back for years.

When you finish applying the strategies I'll share with you in this book, you'll feel more free, open and stronger than before, without the need for habits of the past.

Now that we have established the need for congruency, with all of your communication tools moving in the same direction, we need to consider this: what should you focus on when you speak? What are you aiming to achieve? The answer is one of the great secrets of how to captivate an audience and make your ideas happen. That's what we'll look at next.

To ensure you gain the most value from reading this book, do sign up for the free videos at **www.borntospeak.com/videos** which will support what you learn in the following chapters.

Chapter 2
You were born to feel

I discovered a critical secret to great communication while working with my first big client: a Formula One racing team. The client gave regular presentations to its sponsors, and held meetings with VIPs to help explain the science behind the cars. These helped the sponsors – each giving up to £50 million a year – understand how their money was invested and the value of having their logo on the car. My client invited me to host the meetings in the hope of making the best impression on potential sponsors. I, though, had never watched a Formula One race. In fact, I knew so little about cars that about two weeks before my first meeting with the team, I'd destroyed my own car because the engine didn't have enough water in it. (Yes, I'd ignored the warning lights!) Thankfully, the client told me I would receive an approved script about how the cars were made. I had to memorise the script so that I could deliver it when I met the sponsors.

I will always remember that first meeting. It took me about two weeks to memorise the twenty-page script. Then, when the time came, I stood up in front of about twenty-five people – all of whom had flown over from Germany specially to hear what I had to say – and gave a brief introduction about the history of the team. As I finished the first section of the script, I got a round of applause. Feeling pleased, I continued and, two hours later, at the end, I got another round of applause. The sponsors went off to enjoy lunch.

As soon as they left, the person in charge of hiring me came into the room. He had been watching from outside, through a glass wall. He seemed annoyed: 'What on earth did you say to them?'

This seemed a strange question given that the words themselves had been given to me. 'I just delivered the script that you gave me,' I replied, feeling slightly worried that I might get fired at any moment. He looked confused. 'I don't understand,' he said. 'We've been delivering that same script for years and we've never had a round of applause at the end, let alone at the beginning, what did you do differently?'

I had no idea.

I went away and reflected on what had happened. The more I thought about it, the more I realised that my acting training was paying off. Actors are often told to focus on one specific question in order to deliver the best performance. Business people often ignore or forget that question – but, because of my training, I hadn't.

So what is it? All great communication is essentially guided by three key questions. The first two are automatic – you will apply them whenever you speak. The third question, the most important one, is the one that needs your attention.

The first two are simply:

- What do I want this person to **know**?

- What do I need this person to **do**?

These two questions will inform most of what you say during any meeting. For example, in a job interview, you want the interviewer to **know** that you are the best person for the job. The thing that you want them to **do** is to hire you. Inevitably, everything you say will come down to fulfilling those two objectives. In a sales pitch you might want people to **know** that you have the best product. What you want them to **do** is to make a purchase.

The Formula One team wanted their sponsors to know that it was highly successful at winning races so that the sponsors would keep funding the team year after year. Know and do, right there. However, I approached the meeting wanting to answer one further question.

It seemed to me that my job was to ensure that none of these sponsors felt compelled to take their money and sponsor another team, or sponsor the Olympics, or spend their marketing money on a whole range of other things. My job was to make sure that they felt inspired, excited and compelled to keep sponsoring *this* team. So the extra question I asked myself was 'How do I need these people to **feel**?'

Some people are wary of the notion that we speak in order to make people feel a certain way. Occasionally they say to me, 'This is business! This is no place for feelings!' But, what would happen if clients left a meeting feeling uncertain, disappointed or confused? Most people agree that this would be a bad result. On the other hand, what if clients left the meeting feeling convinced, inspired and motivated? They would **know** what they should **do**, but they would also **feel** compelled to act.

I'm not suggesting that you use cheesy sales tactics to coerce people into acting against their will. I'm talking about connecting with other people in ways that fully engage the logical and the emotional parts of their mind.

The science behind this is clear. As Daniel Kahneman explained in his terrific book *Thinking, Fast and Slow*, the brain has two very important systems. In psychology terms, System 1 is the emotional side and System 2 is the logical side. We often think of ourselves as logical, reasonable people, who make decisions based on facts. In reality, the opposite is true. The parts of the brain that govern our emotions react first to every situation, then they send a message to the logical parts letting them know how we feel about it. If System 1 feels afraid, then System 2 will look for logical reasons for this fear. If we feel excited, our logical mind will search for evidence to explain why we feel this way. In fact, studies show that humans are unable to make decisions if the emotional parts of our brain are damaged.

For example, neuroscientist Antonio Damasio had a patient whom he refers to as 'Elliot'. Elliot was a successful businessman who developed a brain tumour. In order to remove the tumour, surgeons removed a large part of Elliot's orbito-frontal cortex, the area of the brain that connects the frontal lobes with the emotional brain. Elliot lost connection to his emotions. Instead of simply becoming rational, he was unable to make even basic decisions. He could debate if Tuesday or Wednesday would be better for a meeting, but he couldn't make a final decision. This showed how important our emotions are to the

daily decisions we make. Emotions give meaning to facts, allow
to understand how to respond to them. As Damasio wrote, 'We m
describe Elliot's predicament as "to know but not to feel".' Decision
require feelings.

HORNS AND HALOS

In a job interview this is known as the 'horns and halos' effect. When
you first meet someone, you gain an instant feeling about them, bad
or good. In effect, then, in the eyes of the interviewer, the interviewee
gain horns or a halo. Different theories suggest attributing horns or
halos takes anywhere from 5 seconds to 2 minutes. Then, if you like an
interviewee, your logical mind searches for reasons to give him or her
the job. If you take an instant dislike, you'll search for a reason why he
or she would be a poor match for the role. We need facts to back up
our decisions. After all, how could you give an unsuccessful candidate
feedback that they didn't get the job just because you didn't like them
in the first few seconds? Your logic searches for facts to support your
instinct – your feeling – about a person. Outwardly, though, you've
made a completely rational, reasonable and justifiable decision.

Actors are trained to express feelings in a way that moves the
emotions of the audience. After all, no one goes to watch a film or play
in order to see a logical sequence of events. We want to be thrilled,
entertained, saddened, shocked, scared, or uplifted. In short, we want
to feel something.

When I spoke at that first meeting for the Formula One team, I
knew that the script would cover what I wanted the sponsors to **know**
and **do**. My job was to focus on speaking in a way that changed how
they would **feel**.

As an example, recently we had an issue with one of our clients.
They were frustrated with us and demanded a call. It's easy for
situations like this to become worse in the heat of a conversation, and
of course all I really wanted to do was to defend my company and tell
the client how brilliant my team is. However, before the call, I took
a step back and considered what I really needed to achieve from the
conversation. I wanted the client to feel calm and reassured; I wanted

iring the call, I allowed my tone of voice to soothe; nse of collaborative calm. It worked – I eased the iny remained a valued client and now things are ith them.

before your next meeting, conversation or email. ...... you would like people to know during the meeting, what you want them to do after the meeting, and then consider what they need to feel in order to achieve that objective – motivated, energised, disappointed, relieved, grateful, something else? Keep this feeling in mind as you decide what to say and how to say it. The aim is to create a positive resolution for both you and your client, through compassion, concern and collaboration.

We'll get into the specifics of your words and delivery style later on. For now, remember to start with the right intention – connecting as humans, through feelings as well as logic.

ACTION!

Think about an upcoming meeting or conversation. What feeling do you need the other person to have in order to get your desired result? Let the answer to this question guide your tone, your body language and your content.

STOP 'BEING YOURSELF'

All this is very well, of course, but how do you actually change the way that people feel? How do you influence someone's emotions? The most common mistake I hear when people discuss effective communication is that you should 'just be yourself'.

It sounds reassuring (after all, we can all be ourselves), but in fact it's terrible advice. Why? Because we all have a lifetime of bad habits and behaviours that we need to strip away in order to connect with people more successfully.

So, rather than just behaving in a way that currently feels normal it's important to go back, revisit and reset how you communicated when you were habit-free. To revisit a time when you were fully present in your life, more expressive – and more congruent.

In order to understand my own habits, I thought back through my journey from expressive child to awkward teenager and on to self-conscious adult. Suddenly the road that led to my studies in this area became clear.

WHERE DID YOUR ARMOUR COME FROM?

In his now legendary Stanford Commencement speech, Apple founder Steve Jobs said that you should always follow your passions. You won't necessarily know where they may lead, but later on you will be able to connect the dots backwards and see how they created your success.

As I share my own journey, think about your path. Consider the events and turning points that may have shaped how you communicate. This will help you to understand what led you to wear the armour that may now be holding you back.

When I was four years old, I had my first experience of being on stage, as the innkeeper in my school's Christmas nativity. (My parents still have the video to prove it.) I was so thrilled to land the role that I wanted to give it all I had. There was a song that I liked and, even though it wasn't in the script, I asked if I could perform it – solo.

On the day of the nativity, the piano player was ill. The school roped in a last-minute replacement. She had never seen the music and – by the sound of it – I wonder if she had ever actually played the piano before! However, this didn't deter me. I still belted out my song with confidence, to a packed audience. When my crucial innkeeper scene came along, a meek Joseph and Mary shuffled up to me and barely whispered their lines. I proudly announced, at the top of my voice, 'There is no room at the inn... but I do have a stable!' I was a happy, popular kid, who bounced in and out of school – and on and off that stage – with utter confidence. Then, a few weeks before my fifth birthday everything changed. We moved house.

The distance and timing meant that, part-way through the academic year, I had to start a new school. On my first day, I stood outside our house with my older sister for a photo in our new uniforms. I can still remember feeling excited about the adventure of it all.

When we arrived at school, my Mum introduced me to the teacher and I recall looking up at her and feeling wide-eyed and enthused. I remember the classroom vividly.

But then, just a few hours later, my joy had turned to fear and loneliness. I had spent the morning trying to talk to the other children at my table – but nobody responded. I felt ignored. I was sure that I was making sounds loud enough for people to hear me and yet it was as if I didn't exist.

At break time I went to find my sister for comfort. She was happily playing with a new friend on some tyres, the most popular toys in the playground. The two of them asked me to sit on the tyres to 'save' them while they went off for a bit. Inevitably, bigger boys came over and took the tyres from me. Now not only was I invisible, I was also weak and vulnerable and I'd let my sister down.

Back at the classroom, I felt increasingly lost, invisible and rejected. I started shaking and sobbing, and my mind filled with negative questions: why won't anybody listen when I talk? How come they all know how to connect with each other and I don't? What's wrong with me? (Oddly these were the same questions that I would ask myself twelve years later, when my friend bought me the book on body language for my birthday. Until I wrote this book, I hadn't realised I had spent so many years asking myself the same things.) I had gone from feeling popular, happy and safe to friendless, lonely and afraid. And I couldn't understand why.

All humans have an innate need to feel part of a tribe. When we sense that we are isolated or rejected, a primal fear courses through us: if I am rejected, will I have to fend for myself? For earliest humans, isolation would mean almost certain death: it takes a tribe to hunt and therefore a tribe to eat. To avoid danger and survive, we must belong.

It's no wonder, then, that standing up to speak to a group of people creates fear. In doing so, we choose to separate ourselves from those around us, stand out and say, 'Come with me, I know the way.' What if everyone says no? In primeval terms, being rejected puts us at risk.

Think back to your earliest memories. Can you find any moments when you felt unable to express yourself, or when you were rejected or mocked for giving your opinion? These moments may have been the first stages of building the armour you now wear in front of people.

ACTION!

Consider one situation during which you felt rejected. Now look at it with a fresh perspective. Find three positive things that that situation has given you (perhaps it taught you that you have resilience, or has given you greater empathy). Once you can find the positives in your experiences, you will be able to start letting the armour go.

Looking back now, I feel so grateful that this happened to me. If I hadn't had this difficult time switching schools, I may never have felt the concerns that some of my clients feel. Many of those who teach communication have always found it easy to talk to people, so they are less able to relate to clients who don't feel that way. My childhood experiences propelled me to investigate human connection and expression, which I may have otherwise just taken for granted.

I equate the realisation to the ancient understanding of a solar eclipse. I imagine that, at some point thousands of years ago, people took the sun for granted, because it always rose and set each day. Then one day it disappeared. It must have made people question what the sun was, where it came from and whether it would keep on rising and setting. We depend so much on the sun for our survival that we had to be certain that it would continue to be there for us, otherwise our very existence was under threat. In the smallest way, that is how I felt. My ability to connect with my tribe had vanished.

From the age of five I was introduced as, 'This is Richard, he's very shy.' Every time someone said that about me, I felt more embarrassed. I wanted to express myself, but many of my ideas stayed locked inside my head. The fear of being teased and of not being liked, along with my need to fit in made me build up coping mechanisms that shut down my natural ability to speak up and be heard.

For others, bad experiences with communication can go in the opposite direction. Whereas I became introverted, others may hide their embarrassment in bravado and a tough, cold attitude. Their confident or arrogant façade can conceal the fear within – and is just as much a barrier to connection and communication as excruciating shyness can be.

I look at my own children now, who as I write the book are aged six and three, and marvel at their ability to run up to children they've never met before and say, 'Hello, will you be my friend? Let's play together.' These days don't last for everyone. At some point many people form a protective shell and keep others at a safe distance. In fact, I believe that this is one of the greatest challenges we face as a society: there are so many people around us, and yet so many of us rarely feel connected.

ARE YOU HIDING IN PLAIN SIGHT?

By age ten my shell had grown so much that a teacher laughed at me for putting my name down to audition for the school play. She announced to the class, 'I think we've seen everybody that wanted to try out for the lead role in the play, haven't we?'

'No,' I mumbled, 'I put my name down. You haven't called me.'

'Well, yes, we didn't think you would be able to do it. Are you sure you want to have a go?' she retorted.

Yes, I bloody well did! Just because I didn't chatter as loudly as everyone else in the class didn't mean that I shouldn't get a chance. I boldly stepped forward, dusting the cobwebs off my acting skills (my last performance had been the innkeeper) and gave it a shot.

I was given the lead role. I loved every minute of it. Why? I was able to be someone else, someone who knew how to communicate and what to say.

Aged thirteen I took another crack, this time for *Jesus Christ Superstar*. The teacher who auditioned me said that I had looked in pain, almost constipated as I tried to sing. The angst and awkwardness of teenage years had fallen on me so heavily that I could barely get a word out in public without appearing to have a medical condition!

I was given the role of Priest Number 2. In case you're wondering, it isn't a big role, but I was very proud to have four more words in the script than Priest Number 1. That role was given to my closest friend, Christian. He would later go on to perform as a solo artist in front of 36,000 people in London's Hyde Park with the BBC orchestra, as well as appearing in many West End shows. Back then, both of us were hampered by bad habits that had built up after years of trying to survive the battlefield of the school playground.

Five years later, Christian had somehow shed the shackles of those habits, found his voice and would take the lead role in our school's production of *Grease*. I badly wanted to play Kenickie so that we could stand side-by-side and sing 'Greased Lightning' in front of the whole school. This time I was refused an audition. The teacher said, 'No, I think we already know what you're capable of.' I thought this meant they were planning to hand me the role automatically, without even needing an audition, sensing some great talent lurking within me. But no. The casting was announced. My name was not on the list. And I had to watch another guy sing the song I was so desperate to perform, with no apparent regard for the notes or the words.

It felt unfair at the time, but looking back now I can see why it happened. The way that I walked, talked and behaved was closer to a mouse than a lion. Despite being one of the tallest people in school, I acted as if I didn't want to be seen. Gone was the confident four-year-old, who could speak, sing and walk with pride. He had been replaced by a lanky, awkward and tense boy, who kept his thoughts in his head; who lacked the confidence to speak up for himself.

You may have felt the same way at some point. Perhaps you have sat in a meeting and listened to someone spouting crazy ideas that lack any logic. You may have watched everyone else in the room agree with him and his nonsense, while you thought about the twenty better ideas of your own that you assumed no one would hear, even if you spoke up.

The key to being heard in these situations is not to shout the loudest. Nor is it to speak using all the protective habits you've built up since childhood. If you do that, your words and ideas will whimper and squeak rather than roar. You must return to congruency, behaving the way you were born to speak, and focussing on how you want people to feel to motivate them into action.

A few weeks after the curtain closed on the school's production of *Grease* was the week that one of my friends received his rejection letter from Oxford University (the letter that said he couldn't communicate effectively). That tipped me over the edge. Enough was enough. I knew I had to shake myself free of the burden of behaviours that belittled my words before they ever had a chance to fly.

And so I began my journey: first teaching the monks, then studying acting and then presenting for a Formula One team. Now I have spent two decades working as a professional speaker, yet I am still surprised when people say to me at the end of an event, 'You are clearly just so confident at doing this stuff.' I still hear the echoes from my childhood of 'shy boy' and 'Are you sure you want to audition?' bouncing around in my mind.

But this book isn't about me. I have shared these stories simply to let you know that you are not alone. Your past, your habits and the negative voices in your head will not hold you down. No matter what background you come from and what has happened in your life, you too were born to speak.

Reflecting on your own journey (use the questions on the following pages) will help to free your communication style, so that you can behave – and speak – more congruently and authentically and give yourself the greatest opportunity to change how people feel about you and your ideas.

Once you have answered the questions, you can start to get more practical and specific on the few simple changes you can make to enhance your impact, transform your results and improve the reactions you get from a crowd (or an individual) when you speak. All the tips that follow come from scientific research. Undertaking the research wasn't easy, though. In fact, it nearly didn't get off the ground. It was practically laughed out of the room.

Dropping the Armour

The following questions are intended to get you to think about events from your past that could be affecting the way you communicate with other people now. Answer them as fully as you can in the spaces provided.

What events have most challenged or questioned your communication skills – at school, at work, throughout your life? (Think about such things as interviews that may have gone badly; a speech when you felt embarrassed; an event where people teased you for how you spoke; or times when you felt ignored.)

....

....

....

....

....

....

....

....

....

....

How did these events change how you feel about expressing your ideas? What strategies have you developed to help you cope?

....

....

_____

_____

_____

_____

_____

_____

_____

_____

What habits, armour or protective behaviours do you think you need to let go in order to communicate more freely and congruently? (You may discover more answers to this question as you read the book.)

_____

_____

_____

_____

_____

_____

_____

_____

_____

_____

_____

Chapter 3
The science of communication

'It will never work. The reason that this study has never been done is because it cannot be done.' That was the first verdict I received on my idea for a study on influence and communication. The verdict came from Professor Adrian Furnham, Head of Psychology at University College London. And he should know. In his career he has published more than 1,200 academic papers and written seventy books. He is world renowned for his expertise. If anyone knows what will work in a study on behaviour and influence, it's him.

I had been mentally planning the research I wanted to do for a couple of years before we met. Now all that work seemed to be in tatters. I was a laughing stock. He seemed totally bemused by my barmy ideas to study every element of how a person communicated, breaking down the key areas of their non-verbal communication from head to toe. I was aiming too big, too broad, with too many variables. We needed to get more specific.

I spent six months rethinking and redesigning until I finally had a version of the study that would work. I met with the professor again and he agreed to go ahead, but with one final caution: 'It's possible that the study will achieve nothing. You may even get a negative result, showing that the things you are teaching are either useless or unhelpful.' I didn't mind. I just wanted an opportunity to find proof, if there were any. I wanted to identify the most useful behaviours that someone could apply when they stood up to speak. If we could find evidence that certain behaviours gained a better response than others, then I knew that we could teach those behaviours to help people boost the impact of their words and ideas.

What we discovered was far beyond our expectations. When we completed the study, the head statistician said, 'I've been doing this for thirty-five years and it is incredibly rare to see results like these.'

It all started with a simple question: if you behave the way that you were born to speak, are you more likely to inspire, convince and lead people? Could you even sway the results of an election?

The study involved filming someone speaking for about thirty seconds. This may seem short, but we knew that the video didn't need to be any longer, because earlier studies on influence had shown that the evaluation you give a person after thirty seconds is very similar to the ratings you would give them after twenty minutes.

We then gathered a cohort of more than 2,000 people from across Europe, India and North America. Every individual was asked to watch the thirty-second video and evaluate the speaker. The viewers had to give ratings for how inspiring, convincing, knowledgeable and confident the person appeared to be. We also asked how good a leader they felt this person was. Finally, in a yes or no question, we asked if they would vote for the speaker in a political election.

Equal numbers of men and women, aged from eighteen to sixty-five, took part in the study. We wanted to know if people of different ages, nationalities or genders would give different ratings.

Each participant saw only one video. What no one realised was that we had created dozens of different versions of this video. In each version the presenter was asked to do everything in exactly the same way apart from one slight change to body language. We wanted to see whether or not that one change generated a different rating.

We also needed to find out if these changes in body language would work if we changed the speaker's gender, age, skin colour or perceived attractiveness. We used four actors – a man and a woman with fair skin, and a man and a woman with darker skin. In some versions of the video, we aged the actors, using make-up and prosthetics to make each appear roughly thirty years older than their real age. We kept the clothing and words the same in every video. The only differences we were analysing were the movements.

THE SURPRISING RESULTS

Before we ran the study, we imagined that in certain parts of the world, certain stereotypes, as well as sexism and racism, would mean that a fair-skinned, older male might get a far more positive rating as a potential leader than a younger, darker-skinned female.

After the study was completed and thoroughly analysed, we all gathered to discuss the results. With an excited expression on his face, the statistician passed me a sheet of paper. It was filled with numbers that meant nothing to me. I asked what I was supposed to be looking for. Usually a quiet and reflective man, he burst into life.

He explained, 'In order to get a clear result, something that is statistically significant, you need to get a number that is above 1. You've got lots on here that are much higher, you've even got a 16!'

Professor Furnham was also positive. He reassured us that the great quality of our videos meant that we could have equally great confidence in the results.

So, what were they both so excited about? I was hoping to get results that showed something like a 10 percent increase in how convinced someone was by your ideas when you compared one style of speaking versus another. The actual results were quite different.

First, we welcomed the discovery that age, gender and skin colour made no significant difference to the rating. Nor did it matter who watched the videos. Men and women in India had very similar responses to people watching the videos in the USA or Europe.

Then we reached the critical question. Can you walk into a meeting and say the same words and wear the same clothes, but dramatically shift how people rate you and your abilities by a few simple changes in your behaviour?

The data showed us that those using the most effective styles of communication can, compared with the same person using common speaking habits, increase the viewer's opinion of how inspiring and knowledgeable they are by 25 percent. Furthermore, the number of people who believe the speaker is confident increases by 29 percent.

I was stunned. If you read every book ever written, you will know more than someone who has never picked up a book at all. However, people's perception of how much you know can dramatically shift just based on a couple of simple things in your behaviour. This means that the most knowledgeable people may fail to be heard, while those who know relatively little can appear to know more just by the way they behave when they are speaking.

We found that when our speakers let go of bad habits and took on a more effective communication style, 42 percent more people were convinced by their ideas. In effect then, you don't need to change what you say or what you wear if you want to be heard. You simply have to change how you behave. (Of course, having good content is important, but we'll get to that later.)

What about leadership? Whether you lead or manage a team or company, take the lead on a project, or want to gain the respect of the room when you speak, being viewed as a good leader is a highly valuable character trait. We found that small changes to your communication style will increase how confident people feel in your ability as a leader by 44 percent. Same words, same clothes, same person – just a few tweaks on how to communicate.

Finally, we asked if people would vote for the speaker in an election. We were amazed to find that an astounding 58 percent more people would vote for you in an election if you were to avoid common habits of poor communication and instead apply our communication strategies to your speaking style.

In reality, we know that this number would be smaller (after all, when it comes to an election, some people are creatures of habit and will always vote for the same party regardless of any policy or personality; others will vote for policy over style). However, even a 5 percent sway in your favour could be the difference between being elected and not – or, between gaining a job, a promotion or a leadership position and not.

The *Journal of Psychology* published our academic paper in 2016. I was elated. We had proven that any person, no matter their age, race or gender, can dramatically increase their influence on people from a whole range of backgrounds, by behaving the way we were born to speak.

Why is this important? My aim has always been to help great people to do great work. We often see companies, communities and countries being led by the person who just happens to be good at winning votes. I believe that the person with the best ideas and intentions and the greatest ability to create meaningful change should have the means by which to gain support. That can only happen if that person – or those people – have the means by which to communicate effectively.

Ideas will not speak for themselves. You have to do the speaking. If a speaking style puts people off listening to what you have to say, you make the road to achieving your goals that much harder.

So, what exactly was the most effective speaking style we discovered in our research? How exactly were you born to speak?

PART 1
STYLE

Chapter 4
You were born to stand

One of the most painful and enlightening activities in my acting training involved people copying how I walked. I began walking around the room, then another person walked behind me, mimicking and slightly exaggerating my movements. More people joined behind the line and accentuated things further.

I was the first person to take part. I thought the exercise would be boring because I believed I walked normally, with no habits or affectations that I was aware of. I continued walking around the large hall as more people joined the line behind me. I couldn't see what the people behind me were doing, but I could hear the laughter building. When all ten people in our class had joined in, I was told to step away, while they all continued, so that I could see how it looked.

I was appalled. From the first person through to the last I saw a gradual build-up of gangly, feet-scuffing depression. Their necks were jutted forwards, heads looking down and chests caved in. Somehow they were all moving forwards leading with their knees and heads, while the rest of their bodies dragged behind and their feet barely lifted off the floor with each step. It was hard to look at because I realised it was true.

Our research study showed that posture is the first major area you can focus on to transform your impact when you speak. If you revert to the way you were born to stand, you gain more respect and better reactions to your ideas. The challenge, though, is that very few people are aware of how they stand (or sit). Even when you ask people to stand upright, some are tilting backwards, some forwards or sideways. There are habits and tensions around your body that you'll need to become aware of in order to reclaim your natural posture.

I certainly wasn't aware of my walking style. How could this be me? If a toddler tried to walk like this, they would either collapse in a heap or feel too depressed to move. As a proud father of two young boys, I can testify that neither of them has ever behaved that way! Every day they leap out of bed and usually jump on me before dawn, ready for yet another day of running, skipping or bouncing around, all in perfect posture. You don't need dance or movement classes to achieve this as a child. So when does it all go wrong?

First, we start school and are told to sit straight and still. Children even get taught to do this at birthday parties – the magician won't give them a sweet or balloon unless they are sitting silently with their legs and arms crossed. At a birthday party! When they're only five! Where there is sugar and music! So early on, we teach our children obedience and control at the cost of creativity, freedom and expression.

Then, you may recall going through some awkward years at senior school. At this stage of life, you can get picked on for all kinds of reasons, including looking different, working hard or expressing yourself. To avoid being teased we may fall into the trap of pretending not to care, trying to look cool or casual, just to fit in. This can lead to bad habits with your posture, especially when, like me, you're tall.

When I lived in India, the people around the monastery called me *lambo*, which means gangly-giant-man! At school, many of my friends were shorter than me, so I would hunch and slump in my seat in order to stay on eye level with them. I wanted to avoid being the tall poppy who is most likely to have its head sliced off by bullies. I have always loved learning and reading, but these things are often used as reasons to taunt people at school. In an attempt to cover up my studious nature and appear less eager, I learned to walk with minimal effort, wearing down my shoes, which were rarely laced up

(I thought that made me look more casual). I wince thinking back to this, but I can now see it through the lens of survival.

I coach people every day, who, without realising it, have adopted postural habits in order to be liked, accepted, fit in or gain influence. These habits may have helped at school, but in adulthood most of them will almost certainly hold us back.

Think about the transition from student to employee. Some people take the casual, devil-may-care approach. Others realise that their adolescent style just isn't suited to the corporate world, so they take on the affectations of being 'professional'.

When I'm coaching, in order to gain a greater understanding of who my clients are, I ask them what they enjoy doing outside of work. They talk about their children, hobbies or holidays. Almost always, their descriptions of their home life convey far more passion than I hear when they speak about their work. Their bodies open up, their gestures become positive and their faces expressive. So I ask them to speak with the same level of animation about their company or current projects. Many will recoil at the idea – that level of passion for work just doesn't seem professional. Instead, they immediately revert to the stiff behaviour of the workplace.

When we coach junior employees, they often say, 'I would love to express myself, but my boss would never allow it.' When we coach their managers, we hear the same thing in reverse, 'This feels liberating, but my team would never accept it or take me seriously.' It seems that so many people want the freedom to be physically expressive, but everyone is afraid of going first, leading the way towards a new normal. It's time to make a change.

READING PHYSICALITY

In her work at Harvard, social psychologist Amy Cuddy noticed that women are more prone to sit in low power positions than men. More than this, people seem to associate low-power stances with women and high-power with men. She wanted to find out how early this association starts, so she ran an experiment, which she describes in her book, *Presence*. She created images using a wooden, gender-neutral doll, which she placed in different postures. Half the images showed the doll in strong postures, the other half showed weak. She then showed these images to four-year-olds, who were asked which dolls were boys, which were girls. Thirteen percent of the children thought that every strong posture was a boy and every weak posture was a girl.

When she did the same test on six-year-old children, 44 percent felt that all of the strong postures were men and all of the weak postures were women. This means that by age six we are more than three times as likely to see weak postures as female and strong postures as male. This was equally true for all children who took part in the study, boys and girls.

THE CONDITIONING OF CULTURAL SYMBOLS

Why does this happen? The cultural messages we receive about how men and women should behave cause a damaging form of conditioning that happens around the world. We somehow perpetuate the belief that men should take up space and look bold, while women should be small and yielding. These cultural symbols of position and place in the world cause havoc with our natural posture and movements.

For example, many women believe that they are supposed to stand with their feet together, while men are designed to stand with their feet wide apart. This is extraordinary, given that we would never teach this to a child who is learning to walk. When boys or girls are trying to stand for the first time, they continually fall over until they figure out how to balance their weight, with their feet shoulder-width apart, and lift their posture to be perfectly centred.

This perfect posture gives children a natural, physical presence. They can simply stand in front of you, quiet and motionless, and gain the attention of everyone in the room. They have a pure ability to connect.

Then cultural conditions begin to chip away at this instinct. Almost every time we go to a public loo, we see a man represented in a figure that spreads his legs wide like a cowboy-rockstar-hero and a woman in a skirt, standing feet together, looking submissive.

Despite our natural need to stand in an efficient shoulder-width position, by the age of six most girls have come to believe that this powerful stance is not 'natural' for women. They then restrict their stance and movements, losing a crucial part of their presence.

Boys tend to do the opposite, behaving with bravado and taking up too much space, aiming to display the macho dominance they have seen all around them, in action films or on the strangely wide stance of male toilet signs.

Both the very wide and the narrow positions work against our ability to have authentic connection with others. They encourage us to become something that we are not intended to be.

Whether you're male or female, it is highly likely that starting with the cultural expectations associated with your gender and your posture, you have built up a range of physical habits that may limit your ability to speak with influence and impact.

HOW WIDE IS TOO WIDE?

When we talk to our clients about these ideas, the women will often say 'I feel stronger with my feet apart, but I'm not going to do that at work. People will think I'm too masculine.' Men also say that they sometimes like leaning on one hip, crossing their feet or 'standing to attention' with feet together.

When we put together our study videos, we wanted to test how an audience would react to the width of a speaker's feet. And, given that a wide stance is seen as stronger, we wanted to find out how wide is too wide? We asked the presenter to say the same words while standing in three different positions:

- feet together

- feet shoulder-width apart

- feet wider than shoulder-width apart

Take a look at the three images, opposite. Which one of these do you think gained the worst ratings for leadership qualities?

Before the study, we guessed that the position on the right, with feet wider than shoulder width, might get the worst ratings, as it looks ridiculous and abnormal. However, the results showed that you get the lowest ratings for the position on the left, having your feet together.

This doesn't mean you should start standing with your feet as wide as possible. Please don't! Several British politicians have been photographed doing this and it looks absurd. But, when it comes to leadership, despite the absurdity of the very wide-apart stance, having your feet together is even less convincing.

The narrow stance is seen as subservient. There's nothing necessarily wrong with that: if you want to show subservience (and there are times when that's appropriate), it's the right stance to use.

The position that our study showed was most likely to make you look like a leader was the shoulder-width stance. We were staggered by what a difference this made. There was a 32 percent increase in the number of people who said they would vote for you in an election, simply based on going from feet together to feet shoulder-width apart. We found this to be true no matter the age, nationality, race or sex of the presenter or of the audience. Belief in the person who stands with their feet shoulder-width apart is universal.

So why on earth would that one small change make such an enormous difference?

TRIBE LEADER

We are tribal creatures. In a tribe we feel safe. We want to be led by people who seem strong enough to stand up to challenges. If you stand with your feet too close together, you are a push-over, literally.

Try standing with your feet together and ask someone to push you sideways – if you don't instantly fall over, you will certainly wobble. If you stand with your feet too wide, you are in a stronger position, but your movements are restricted (and it looks strange!). However, if you stand shoulder-width, you have gravity on your side. You are physically balanced and in a strong stance, ready for action.

So the first step you can take towards behaving the way you were born to stand is to literally step sideways. Place your feet apart. Stand in a strong, balanced position. Own your space. It is yours to have or give away. You were born to stand this way. You did it naturally as a child. You owned your space and had tremendous presence. You can do this again as an adult, just by giving yourself permission. It may feel odd at first, fighting a lifetime of standing habits, but soon you will come to love it and it will feel totally natural again.

DON'T 'STAND LIKE A MAN', STAND LIKE A HUMAN

When we published our study, it featured in lots of national media. Articles about it popped up in the *Daily Mail*, *Stylist* magazine and the *Daily Telegraph*. Unfortunately, none of these articles embraced the point of the study, which is that all men and women are born to stand like this and the science proved this stance works equally well for us all, regardless of gender, skin colour or age.

Some of the media went with the title 'Women who want to succeed should stand like a man.' This is totally false. While our male-dominated society may have created expectations for women to stand feet together, in a weaker position, this is not how you were born to stand. Women are subject to the laws of gravity in the same way that men are.

We have worked on our stance techniques with clients in Shanghai, Singapore, San Francisco, South Africa and everywhere in between.

The results are always the same. Men and women who stand with their feet shoulder-width apart are more convincing and engaging.

You don't have to look far to find plenty of female examples. Beyoncé may move around the stage at her concerts, but when its time for a strong delivery she will stand centred. In the acting world, Julia Roberts and Emma Watson can often be seen walking down the red carpet, then turning to face the cameras for photos, standing nicely balanced with their feet shoulder-width apart. Take a look at HRH Queen Elizabeth II. Even when she was younger, talking to children, she would gracefully stand in a strong, shoulder-width position, which she still maintains today. In fact, a member of the Queen's staff once saw a talk I gave in London. He was so impressed by my description of the Queen's posture (and the rest of the talk) that he invited me for tea at Buckingham Palace!

Masculine and feminine – becoming more of you

We all have masculine and feminine qualities. There are many different descriptions and definitions of what this means. A wider stance doesn't make you manly, it just allows you access to a certain aspect of your personality. Later on we will talk about movement and gestures. Some have suggested that these are more feminine qualities. No matter how you define them, it is important to embrace them all. Accessing both sides of yourself won't make you seem boyish or girly. It will make you appear more human.

DYNAMIC STILLNESS

I first heard about dynamic stillness during my acting training. It baffled me. How could you be dynamic without moving? I constantly wanted to show how hard I was working on stage in order to try and please my teachers and the audience, so I would move around a lot, employing every muscle in my body and face at all times.

Directors would then tell me to move less and trust stillness. They said that if I stood with great posture and spoke the words with the correct emotional tone, then the message would travel. In order to achieve gravitas, I would need to think about actors such as

Sir Anthony Hopkins, Dame Judi Dench or Morgan Freeman, who could walk on stage or screen, speak lines in complete stillness and win awards for how captivating they were.

As proof of this, Judi Dench once said that she lived in constant fear that she would get fired, because she felt she wasn't doing anything. She always left her bag near the door of a rehearsal room, so that she could make a quick exit if someone complained about how little effort she made. She explained that great communication feels like doing nothing – being present, listening and reacting.

Of course, standing still is not enough. Sometimes you'll need to move. But when you are still, the position you're standing in can make a big difference. One thing that makes great actors stand out from others is how they interact with gravity. Most people have small and subtle habits in their behaviour when they stand up to give a presentation or speech, which reduce or remove their gravitas.

There are three stances that are most common, which I am sure you have seen in action.

The Lean

In a bid to look calm, feel comfortable and feign relaxation, many people stand with their weight rested on one foot or the other. They have their hip off to one side, as if they are out for drinks with friends.

This may work well socially, but if you're speaking to a room of colleagues or clients it may work against you. If you lean your weight to one side, you are not standing in a position of balance and readiness, but in a position of weakness. Think back to the earlier point about know, do, feel. When you speak to people in this leaning position, they may logically **know** what you want them to **do**, but may **feel** that you are a push-over and ignore your ideas.

We often learn about working with gravity when playing a sport. At school I loved playing basketball. My team was considered exceptional in the history of our school, as no other team had won so many games. We were the county champions and in our final year, we beat every other team by at least 30 points. It helped that most of our school team also played together on Saturdays in the national league, where we gained extra coaching. We were all taught the importance of gravity and posture when shooting the ball. One day, the coach asked me to take a free-throw. As I got ready to shoot, he placed one hand gently on my shoulder and pushed me over. I fell flat on my face. I was shocked, but he explained that you can't shoot a ball accurately when your body isn't balanced. We learned that to improve our shooting accuracy, we had to stand strong, centred and grounded, with our feet shoulder-width apart, otherwise the ball could drift in one direction or another.

I was later taught the same strategy when learning tennis and golf. If you look at the best players in any of these sports, men or women, you will see them doing the same. Before a key moment in so many sports, the athlete will pause and stand with their feet shoulder-width apart, and in doing so prepare to take their best shot.

The Sway

After a while the leaning position becomes uncomfortable, with all of your weight focussed on one hip, so you have to alternate sides. Some people extend this movement into swaying back and forth. This can have a calming quality for a speaker, reminding us of times when we were a baby being rocked to sleep by our parents. However, when the audience sees a repetitive swaying motion, like a pendulum or a hypnotist's watch swinging back and forth, it sends them to sleep!

Women tend to do this movement from one hip to the other, whereas men will often lift up the toe of their shoe, rocking back onto the heel. You may even catch men looking at their shoe as they deliver an important message, entranced by their own movements!

What feels good to you may not look good to the people who are watching you. Your body and voice are a vessel for your message and you need to deliver your words in a way that is most convincing for the audience, not that feels most comfortable for you.

In our study, we found that the lowest scores by far were given to speakers who used a swaying motion.

Aim to remove any distracting or repeated patterns in your posture and movement. You may not be aware of doing them, so try filming yourself or ask for feedback from a colleague. You may be surprised by how many unnecessary shifts you're making as you speak!

The James Dean

Some people claim to be centred and still, but there is one more trap to look out for. The most common position I see people standing in is what I call the James Dean 'too-cool-for-school' look.

At school, in an effort to look like you were laid back, you may have fallen into the backwards slouch. This is where you plant your feet, but lean your top half back slightly.

During my coaching sessions, I frequently see people trying hard to appear casual when they talk, as if they don't need approval for their presentation. However, if you're leaning backwards, gravity is working against you: if someone gave you a nudge, you would fall over. It's out of balance, so it's physically weak.

As a side note: if you're someone who uses this posture as a form of protection, as a means to convince people that you're unsure of your ideas (so that if it turns out they're unsure, it's okay – because you agree with them), you will never motivate or convince your audience. Who wants to be led by someone who looks like they struggle to stand up for their ideas?

ADJUSTING YOUR PHYSICAL PRESENCE

There are a few activities you can do to reset your posture, and in doing so increase your presence and gravitas.

1. Find your centre

You'll need a friend or partner to help you with this. Your aim is to find out where to place your feet to feel balanced, steady and strong.

- Stand with your feet together, so that they are touching and your weight feels centred.

- Ask your friend to stand at your side and, using as little force as possible, put one hand on your shoulder and push you gently over sideways.

Your friend should need hardly any effort. Your feet are in a weak place: you're like a thin, rootless tree, blown down by a gentle breeze.

- Now shift your feet so that they are shoulder-width apart. This may feel too wide for you at the moment, that's okay.

- Find your centre of balance and check that you're physically centred between your left foot, right foot, toes and heels.

- Consciously look for any tension in your body, and relax. Aim to keep your body relaxed throughout.

- Now ask your friend to push you, using the same force as before. How do you feel?

You should feel much stronger in this second position. Even if your friend pushes harder, you should be able to stay in place with little effort. Your muscles aren't more powerful. Gravity is just working more effectively on your body, giving you greater strength. In an onlooker's eyes, the position also gives you greater gravitas.

Now, in your daily life, look for the habits that have become your posture preferences – probably to lean towards one side or the other, perhaps slightly forward onto the balls of your feet, or backwards onto your heels. Consciously acknowledge how you stand. You don't have to avoid standing like this all the time – just become aware of it so that you can shift into a stronger position when you need to.

ACTION!

When you have something to say that you want heard, make a conscious effort to centre your body, so that you have gravity – and gravitas – on your side.

2. Practise 'Hands, Heels, Head'

Years of hunching over computers, desks and phones leads many of us to fall into the habit of slumping. The 'Hands, Heels, Head' technique lets you lift your posture back up to its full height. I remember doing this when I was working at the Royal Albert Hall in London. I was standing on stage while the technicians were preparing the camera equipment. I could see an image of myself on a massive, cinema-sized screen and I didn't like what I saw: I looked flat and downbeat. I checked my posture – I was centred, feet placed nicely apart, but somehow I seemed crumpled.

That's when I did the 'Hands, Heels, Head' activity. When I looked back at the screen, I saw a different image. I seemed more confident, proud and inspired. Once you get used to checking yourself in this way, you'll fix your posture in a matter of seconds. Here's how:

- Place your feet shoulder-width apart and check that your weight is centred between your toes, heels, left and right feet. Allow your arms to hang naturally by your sides. Relax.

- Slowly reach your arms out sideways, higher and higher, until they are outstretched, with your hands high above your head.

- Reach higher with your hands so that you go up on your tiptoes. Tilt your head backwards and look up to the ceiling with the aim of reaching a little higher with your whole body.

- Once you're as high as you can go, start to come down in the following way. First, just drop your hands down so that they are by your sides again.

- Next, just drop your heels down, so that your feet are flat on the floor, but your body is still lifted.

- Then just drop your head forwards, bringing it back to its centre, so that you are looking straight ahead.

You may feel as though you have just grown a good few centimetres taller! This lifted posture is closer to the way children stand when they are excited or proud. You did it naturally when you were a child, too (and that's why it probably feels so good). Importantly, it looks great to an audience. Don't force it, with a puffed-up chest. You should feel lifted, free and in natural alignment.

Once you're in a centred, strong and lifted position, you'll be able to deliver a confident and compelling talk, feeling good and appearing more convincing. This is your ready position. You don't have to stay like it, you can move around as needed (we'll discuss this later), but like a great sports person you need to start from a position where you are primed to perform at your best. Sports people, Hollywood stars, royalty and even superheroes – they all use this stance to look and feel confident.

(Take a seat if you're still standing.)

It may take a while to get used to standing in this way again, so I recommend daily practise until it feels natural. Actors often say that an amateur will practise until he gets it right, but professionals practise until they can't get it wrong.

From Clark Kent to Superman

Whether you're sitting or standing, there's one extra tip on posture that's worth keeping in mind when you speak about something important. I'll explain it as if you're sitting down, but you can apply it equally well if you're standing.

3. Get centred when sitting down

You'll need a stright-backed chair for this exercise – a dining-room or office chair will do. Not an armchair!

- Sit towards the front of the seat. Put your feet flat on the floor and ensure you're not leaning against the back of the chair, but are supporting yourself, sitting upright.

- Gradually, tilt your upper body forwards, then backwards until you find a position that feels central, with gravity pulling straight down on you. In this position you're just going to test out one small move that can make a huge difference in visual impact.

- Locate your sternum, the hard, flat bone in the centre of your chest. Drop it inwards and downwards, so that you hunch and droop slightly, with your shoulders and stomach forwards and your chest caved in.

- Now lift your sternum upwards and forwards, a little at a time, until you feel that your chest is proud and lifted. Don't overextend so that you feel puffed up – just gently lifted.

When you go from a position of lowered sternum to lifted sternum, your impact goes from defeated to victorious. What's more, if you stay in this lifted position long enough, you'll actually start to feel more victorious. That's because your mind and body are intricately connected. Your mind will remember the times in the past when you naturally adopted this position because you felt inspired or proud. The lowered position triggers a muscle memory of moments when you felt depressed, beaten or negative.

Christopher Reeve, the actor who played Superman in the movies during the 1970s and 1980s, showed us how powerful this shift can be. In the original 1978 movie, Clark Kent, Superman's bumbling and apologetic alter-ego, wears rather bland clothing. When the world needs a hero, he goes into a phone booth (possibly the worst place you could find to change your clothes!) and puts on his cape and tights and emerges as Superman. In the most obvious way, this is how we (the audience) notice the shift. But is it the only way?

There's one scene in the movie during which the change from Clark Kent to Superman is through posture alone. Clark comes to collect Lois Lane for a date, walking in with a low sternum and jangly arms (and speaking in high-pitched voice). When she leaves the room, he lifts his sternum and immediately appears to be Superman – no change of clothing required. The moment she comes back into the room, he drops his sternum and he's Clark Kent again.

Don't go too far with this position, though. Keep it subtle – you don't want to overshoot Superman and end up looking like the Hulk! Think pride, not arrogance. Inspired, not inflated.

When you combine the centred stance with the lifted sternum you may feel strange at first, but remember this is exactly how you were born to stand (or sit). This is your 'ready position'. You will feel so much better and your audience will thank you for it.

Now that you're strong and centred again, we need to think about your movements, because some of them will win positive attention, while others are fatal distractions.

Chapter 5
You were born to move

'Sit still, don't move and repeat after me!' These were the instructions given to the children at the local Tibetan school in Kalimpong, where I taught English in between lessons with the monks. The other teachers threatened children with canes and hit them if they didn't comply. They wrote words on blackboards for the children to repeat in robotic chants.

One day, I entered a classroom and saw a list of countries and capital cities on the board. I thought I would do a quick, fun check to see who could remember what they had learned.

'Okay, who can tell me the capital of France?' Silence. Fear. Confusion. It was on the blackboard, in clear writing. The children were bright and able to read, but none of them knew the answer.

'Can you read this sentence?' I suggested softly, pointing to the board. In unison they said, 'The cap-it-al of France is Pa-ris.'

'Terrific,' I said. 'So who can tell me what the capital of France is?' Silence again. Worried faces. They had no idea. Motionless chanting under threat of being caned wasn't helping them to learn. It just taught compliance.

My lessons were different and caused quite a stir. They were loud, active and physical. One of my favourites was teaching prepositions. I needed the children to learn the following: up, down, into, onto, over, under, out, in front, behind, next to, opposite, round and round about. We performed each through actions that matched the words, so that the children could remember them – years later.

When I was an actor, people would often ask me how I remembered all the lines. They pictured me sitting and reciting them aloud. But, like many actors, I learnt them physically, acting out the scene and allowing muscle memory to embed the words in my mind.

My first paid acting job required a different skill, though. It was a sixty-second Austrian commercial. The scene had to convey the following story: a young man and woman enjoy a date together and go back to her apartment. She suggests that he should stay the night and he agrees. Then, he remembers that he has some errands to run and must get to the bank before it closes. She reassures him that he can do online banking with her computer. He is delighted, does what he needs to do, and then relaxes to enjoy the rest of the evening. The whole story had only four spoken words: '*Ich muss zur bank*' ('I must go to the bank'). Everything else was conveyed through our movements and expressions.

This is the oldest skill in the actors' repertoire. Before talking pictures existed, the likes of Buster Keaton and Charlie Chaplin conveyed a feature-length story in silence. Yet, still we laughed, gasped and sighed. Marilyn Monroe said that the difference between her civilian self, Norma Jean, and her movie-star persona came down to how she moved. She could hide in plain sight and then switch styles to gain attention when she wanted to.

More recently, Pixar's movie *Wall-E* has no dialogue in the first thirty-nine minutes. It gained six Academy Award nominations, equalling the most for an animated film. In 2011, *The Artist* won Best Picture, and also Best Actor for Jean Dujardin, even though he barely spoke in the entire movie. I'd like you to keep all this in mind when you think about communication. Actions speak louder than words. If you want to move people, consider how you move yourself.

You may have seen terrific speakers, motivators and comedians bounding back and forth around the stage to excite and entertain an audience. Should you do the same? How do you need to move in order to gain and hold people's attention?

Before humankind had words, our species used the body to gain understanding from and collaborate with different tribes. If you don't use your body to express yourself, you shut off a very powerful form of communication that resonates with people the world over. The type of movements you make can create a huge difference in your impact. Some are very useful, while others are just…

FATAL DISTRACTIONS

You may have noticed that speakers who move around a lot are effective sometimes and annoying at others. To gain clarity on this, let's talk about what **not** to do.

Some people wander around because they think it's the only way to gain attention. In those situations the movements are just masking other problems with content or delivery. Look at it this way, if your president or prime minister stood deadly still and told you there'd been an attack and your country was going to war, you wouldn't think 'I stopped listening because you were standing still, could you say that again and move around a bit?'

If you want to win attention, your content needs to be meaningful. You can use your voice and gestures to reinforce and emphasise key points, but aimless wandering serves no purpose.

What about comedians? Some seem to run a marathon while on stage. Random movements are jester-like, which is completely fitting for comedy. But what happens when comedians deliver punchlines? They stand still. The impact of the joke is greater, because the audience is able to focus on the most important message.

Now let's meet Pacey, Bobby and Elvis, the most distracting movements that people often make.

Pacey

Back in the days of cavemen, we needed good survival instincts to stay alive. One that proved highly useful is 'fight, flight or freeze'. Faced with a threat, we could make a choice – attack, retreat or hide. We still have this survival mechanism. It comes out whenever we are in danger or anxious, including when we find ourselves standing in front of a room full of people, their eyes fixed on us, like lions hunting a lamb. Some people stiffen up, hoping not to be noticed. Many others turn into Pacey and go into fight or flight mode. And sometimes both modes at the same time.

Pacey starts walking towards his audience, in a show of enthusiasm, confidence and fearlessness. Then he retreats awkwardly back towards the presentation screen, before powering forwards again. Pacey thinks that he is being visually engaging and dynamic, but all the audience sees is someone moving backwards and forwards in a way that bears no relationship to the words he is speaking! This makes it much harder to pay attention to Pacey's ideas.

Everything we see goes through the optic nerve, the largest nerve in our body. In fact, it is not really a nerve – it is an extension of the brain. It is twenty times larger than the nerve we use for hearing. Therefore, if you make unnecessary movements when you speak, you will distract people from what you're saying. In effect, if you move your legs for no reason while you talk, the message people receive is:

'Let me give you an update **<legs moving>** on our finances **<legs moving>** from the last quarter **<legs moving>** **<legs moving>** so that we can **<legs moving>** make the **<legs moving>** right decision about **<legs moving>** what to do **<legs moving>** next...'

I'm not suggesting that you stand still all the time, but don't walk around for no reason. Take control, feel settled and centred. Only move when you need to.

Bobby

Some people do a miniature version of Pacey, called Bobby. Bobby stands in one place, but in order to relieve the fight or flight mechanism, he bobs up and down. He may bob up onto his toes as he gets excited or inspired about a point he is making, then bob back down when he loses enthusiasm. This movement serves no purpose other than offering Bobby some comfort. Try to avoid becoming Bobby. Listeners will thank you for it and your message stands a far greater chance of being heard.

Elvis

In the working world, most conversations, interviews and meetings happen sitting down. Legs are tucked safely underneath a table, so what harm could they do? Keep an eye on Elvis!

Elvis is a shifter. When we're sitting down and feel uncomfortable, nervous or awkward about what we're saying, we start moving our legs and shifting in our seats. The effect is clearly visible throughout our posture: Elvis swings back and forth, diminishing the impact of his words just when he needs people to listen. Keep your legs still when you have something important to say. You will feel more calm and appear more confident.

ACTION!

Choose your movements based on how you want people to feel. Move with purpose to help your listeners understand or catch the mood of what you're saying; stay still for key statements that require impact.

'WHAT SHOULD I DO WITH MY HANDS?'

This is the most common question I get asked by people who are preparing for an important presentation, interview, speech or pitch. In a way it's a funny question to ask. After all, you don't normally have any problem with your hands, do you? It's not as if you would meet your friends in a bar at the end of the week, with limp arms dangling and flapping at your sides and say, 'Could somebody hold my drink? I don't seem able to use my hands!'

You move your arms and hands freely all the time. You tell stories and paint pictures with your gestures. You do it naturally and don't even think about it. The challenge comes in high-pressure situations when you get self-conscious. You lose the ability to move naturally. You have no idea how you would normally move and so you might gesture too much or keep your hands frozen still and end up feeling stifled. You just need to get back into a natural rhythm. You can reawaken your instinct for what to do with your hands by keeping a few key principles in mind.

Variety and congruency

I was once asked to coach the CEO of a software company. He was a South African guy who was very formal, firm and slightly aggressive in the way that he spoke. I watched him practise delivering a presentation in front of his team. While he had good things to say, he was stilted and wooden.

I suggested that he add some movement, to free himself up and bring the message to life. In response he started moving one arm around like a windmill. It didn't help! When we discussed it, he admitted he was worried about dropping his fierce exterior in case his team stopped taking him seriously. I explained that the lack of variety along with the tension in his movements made him hard to watch. If he had the courage to move freely, his perceived authority would go up, not down. We could all tell that the way he was moving was unnatural. This was a learned behaviour to protect himself from the threats, judgements and challenges that a CEO faces.

We took a bold step out of his comfort zone. I asked him to read a children's storybook, while gesturing as if speaking to his daughter. His face came to life, his arms created vivid images and his voice captivated us. Then he went back to his work presentation. It was transformed. His team told him that they felt lit up with inspiration from him, cared for and ready to put his ideas into action.

Many people assume that keeping their arms still will increase their gravitas. While keeping your legs still can be helpful, it doesn't work the same way for your arms. When you want to describe something, you naturally move your arms. You move them less for serious situations, more when you're excited or happy, but either way you move them.

Dr Susan Goldin-Meadow did a lot of research in this area at the University of Chicago. She found that moving your arms while talking improves your brain function, making you a better communicator. It helps your mental coherence, increases the efficiency of your speech and stimulates your memory. She conducted a study involving seventy-two mathematicians who were asked to describe how they had solved an equation. Those who were told to gesture were able to recall and describe their solutions far more accurately than those who were told to keep their hands still. Gestures are not just useful for your listeners, they are critical for mental coherence.

That doesn't mean it's easy! Stress, habit or feeling self-conscious can restrict your natural power to communicate with your arms. When I first started working with our Formula One client, I had no idea how to move my arms, so I just kept them still. Then, when I realised it was weakening my impact, I researched possible solutions. I was speaking to people from all over the world, so I needed to use gestures that would work internationally.

Research shows that some elements of body language are learned, some are inborn. Learned signals vary from one culture to the next. Thumbs up, thumbs down and the 'okay' symbol (thumb and forefinger in a circle) can mean different things in different countries. However, inborn signals are the same all over the world.

Handshakes have the same impact as gestures

Imagine someone walking towards you, wanting to shake hands with you. Their hand is outstretched, but their palm is facing downwards towards the floor. They put their hand on top of yours as they shake it. What impression are they trying to make? Most people say this is a display of dominance, as if that person is trying to show that they are more important than you.

Look at this again in reverse. If your hand is palm up, at the bottom of the handshake, how do you feel? Most say that this feels weak and submissive.

Now consider this: how does it feel when someone uses both arms to shake hands with you? I hear a whole range of responses to this. Some say it feels controlling; others think it feels warm; still others, sleazy. All of these may be true. The second hand is an amplifier. This means that it amplifies whatever you're saying with the rest of your body language. Putting a hand on someone's shoulder when you shake hands with palm downwards amplifies the dominance. We tend to use only one hand when we first meet someone. When you know someone well the second hand can add warmth.

Why does this matter? It matters because it is the simplest way to remember how to gesture. In future, when you're wondering what to do with your hands, imagine that you're shaking hands with the people or person you're talking to.

- Palms-down gestures emphasise dominant statements.
- Palms-up gestures are for open messages or questions.
- Using two hands amplifies the message.

Palms down

Imagine that you're delivering a talk and half-way through someone objects or questions the reliability of the information you're giving. Here are two ways you might respond:

- Option 1: with your palms facing up and your shoulders lifted, say, 'I'm sure these facts are correct.'
- Option 2: with your palm facing downwards, push gently away from you and say, 'I'm sure these facts are correct.'

Which one feels more strong and certain? No matter where I'm coaching, whom I'm coaching, or what I'm coaching, I can tell you that almost every person in every part of the world agrees that Option 2 is stronger. Palms down is a gesture that we use to show certainty, or make strong, confident statements. You could use palms down to say:

- 'That's my final offer.'
- 'We must have this finished by four o'clock on Thursday.'
- 'We are the best company to work with on this project.'

It's a universal symbol for a closed statement, a strong message, when there are to be no arguments or questions. It conveys that your listeners simply need to feel certain and act on what you say.

Palms up

On the flip side, sometimes you need to show warmth and openness, and invite other people to give their opinions. That's when you can use palms up. This is perfect as a gesture when you want to say and reinforce the message:

- 'Welcome to the meeting.'

- 'What do you think we should do?'

- 'I'm not sure.'

When you want questions, discussion and feedback from your audience, use palms up. I have seen so many leaders in team meetings and conferences say, with palms down, 'Do you have any questions?' The palms-down gesture implies that they don't want any questions, so the audience stays silent. If you want to engage people, encourage them to talk and share ideas, show this visually with palms up. In short, when you're aiming to control the input and interaction from a group of people, palms up means 'speak up' and palms down means 'shut up'. Your audience will respond to this no matter where they are from.

We have all seen this in action in the theatre. Last year I took my two young boys into London to see *Dick Whittington*. It was around Christmas and there were 3,000 eager and overexcited children and exhausted parents in the audience. Many of the kids had big buckets of popcorn, sweets and fizzy drinks and were squealing in a caffeine and sugar frenzy before the play even began!

When the hero walked on stage and gestured vigorously with palms up, the kids jumped out of their seats yelling and cheering, popcorn flying in all directions. But then the hero gestured palms down and they were instantly silent. I watched the parents around me. Many looked in awe as their overexcited kids were finally still. How had the actor performed such magic? He literally had every child in the palm of his hand.

Handle questions as if you are directing traffic

A few years ago I was working in Atlanta. I left the conference venue to go for a walk and reached a major road junction. There were four lanes of traffic going north, four going south, four going west, four going east. Sixteen lanes of traffic. And the traffic lights had failed.

To save the cars from chaos, there was a traffic cop in the middle of the junction. She looked no bigger than five feet tall. Armed with nothing more than hand signals and a whistle, she expertly guided those sixteen lanes of traffic in perfect harmony. How? Palms up for 'go' and palms down for 'stop'.

You can use exactly the same method with a group of people who want to ask questions, raise objections or debate an issue. If you get interrupted in a meeting, you may feel flustered. You may step back in retreat mode, step forward in attack mode or just freeze and lose the confidence of the room and the control of the discussion. It doesn't have to be this way. No matter how heated a discussion becomes and how many voices are involved, you can just react like the Atlanta traffic cop, in a business-like fashion.

When the first person asks a question, turn towards them with your palm up, as if to invite them to speak. If other people try to interject, turn to them with a brief palm down (note – not toward their face, but a gentle palm down towards the floor or table, in their direction). This lets them know that you acknowledge that they would like to speak and will come back to them. Allow the first person to talk and when you have dealt with that person, turn to the next person and invite them to speak with palms up. This ensures that you are properly facilitating the discussion, giving people a focal point and a place to channel their views. To finish the discussion you can do so with palms down and a final statement.

These simple signals are universal. They are strong, clear, easily understood and will guide everyone on how to behave.

Double your impact

When you're talking to one person, sitting down, you may not need both hands. You can do palm up or palm down with one hand, as well as a whole range of other gestures to visually describe a message.

Use your second hand as reinforcement. Using both hands palms down adds strength and closure to a message. Using both palms up is more welcoming, encouraging people to speak up in a discussion, or you can use it to express openly your uncertainty about an issue.

If you're speaking to a larger crowd, you may need to use that second hand more often, to visually engage the whole group.

Size matters

When I did my first performance in a professional theatre, the director kept on saying, 'Bigger, wider, louder!' every time we rehearsed a scene. I couldn't understand why. I was certain that my acting was credible and authentic. I felt connected with the people on stage. Why couldn't he see that?

He asked the entire cast to go up to the highest, farthest row of the theatre. There were 1,000 seats, on three levels. The director remained on stage with two actors. They looked like ants in human clothing.

He began by saying, 'This is how you have been performing so far.' The actors were told to do the scene for us. We could barely see them, let alone hear them or feel anything from their delivery.

'Let's try that again,' he said, 'but this time… bigger, wider, louder.' They repeated the scene and we were transfixed. Same words, same actors, but the impact was transformed. Rather than speaking at a level that suited them, they were communicating at a scale that matched the needs of the audience.

We spend most of our time talking to one person, perhaps two at a time. We aren't used to speaking to larger groups. Even if you make regular presentations, you'll spend the majority of your time talking to individuals (or nobody at all, in a world where we rarely meet others and simply rely on emails and phone calls). What feels natural for you, what works in an intimate space, won't work when you speak to a crowd. Your muscle memory will make you gesture in a way that is appropriate for one person rather than many.

To fully engage people, the size and scale of your movements must reflect your audience. Look at the size of the group and make your gestures as wide as the people in it for inclusive statements, such as 'welcome…', 'thank you…', or 'does anyone have any questions?' You can make smaller gestures too, just be aware that you need to visually and vocally adapt to the space you're in.

How big is a number?

The size of your gestures can also help people understand the value of your numbers. For example, in some situations the statistic 3 percent could be huge, in others it could be tiny. It might convey good news in some situations, bad news in others. Your gestures will help people know what you mean. Try this:

Put your hands wide apart and say, 'If you invest £100,000 in this project...'. Now, put your hands close together and say, 'you'll get a 10 percent return on your money.' It seems like it's a bad deal. There's not much point in investing – the £100,000 was big and the return was small. Now, try this:

Put your hands close together and say, 'If you invest £100,000 in this project...' (now open your hands wide and continue) 'you'll get a 10 percent return on your money.' This seems like a much better deal. Same words, different gestures, opposite meanings.

I've seen countless people bring their hands close together in a tiny gesture and say something along the lines of, 'We are a huge company and have delivered amazing results for our clients.' Then, turned their palms upwards and, shrugging, concluded, 'I'm sure we can do the same for you.' Not very convincing, is it?!

I'm not in the business of making you more influential for the sake of it. I just want to make sure that people fully understand your ideas. I want you to communicate your message so clearly and congruently that if you were in a monastery in India, talking to monks who spoke no English, they would understand the essence of what you said.

Politicians' gestures

After almost every talk I give, people queue up to ask questions. Many of those questions ask me to decode why this politician or that politician makes a certain, odd-looking gesture.

And most of the time, I agree that the politician's gesture (whomever he or she is and whatever the gesture) is odd. I am very much against the type of coaching that some politicians have had. Often it leads to unnatural behaviours that make us suspicious.

Lots of people used to ask me about Bill Clinton. A very charismatic politician, Bill Clinton knows how to work a room. However, when he was President, he had a habit of clenching a fist, with a thumb on top of it, when he was giving a speech. He would jab the thumb at people as he spoke. I understand he was coached to do this in order to avoid a more aggressive finger-wagging. But it looks odd. Would you gesture that way when speaking to your friends? No. Then it's not going to work. As soon as people spot an unnatural behaviour it becomes a distraction and they stop listening to your message.

Descriptive gestures

You make thousands of gestures every day. When you free your arms to move as you speak, they will find a flow. That natural flow will lead to descriptive gesturing – arm and hand movements that describe what you're saying, that paint the pictures of your words.

Keep looking out for these and you will notice them more and more. You, and others, will use them when you feel most at ease to express your opinion. If you increase your awareness of them, you'll find it easier to create a natural flow when you're under pressure.

Frequency of gesturing

Vanessa Van Edwards did some research on TED talks to find out if the most popular speakers had anything in common. Her team analysed every talk given in 2010. The most significant data they came across was that the most popular speakers gestured twenty-six times per minute. The least popular speakers gestured only fifteen times per minute. The team also researched Presidential inauguration speeches. Barack Obama used around twenty-four gestures per minute at his first inauguration, thirty-three per minute at his second. John F. Kennedy used thirty-three per minute too.

More is not necessarily a good thing, though. It can become too much. Donald Trump used forty-three gestures per minute in his inauguration speech. He is among the few people I would encourage to gesture less. Consider it this way: most people talk at a rate of around 2.5 words per second. Good speakers are gesturing roughly every five to six words to emphasise the key words in a sentence. If you gesture more than this, you become overly emphatic, as if claiming that every word is important.

Gestures add visual reinforcement and emphasis for your voice. A couple of gestures per sentence will hit the key words and people will more easily understand what you're saying.

Keeping your hands ready for action

What happens when you're not gesturing? You need a resting place, where your hands are ready for action. Putting them behind your back is no good. Nor is sitting on them (keep them visible at all times). Holding them limply together below your waist appears de-energised.

Look at television presenters. You'll notice that most of them do the same thing. When they're not gesturing, they rest their hands together in a middle position, just above their waist. Put your arms out in front of you, clap your hands together and pull them in towards your belly button. That's where they need to be. If you're wearing a belt, your hands should rest above this. It may feel strange at first, but looks great.

What does the science say?

When we conducted our own study, we didn't just focus on feet. We also considered five different gestures. On the opposite page there are drawings of the gestures we wanted to test. This is what we found:

- Top left. Avoid this one. Half-hearted gestures, limply flapping arms by your sides but never bringing them above your waist got the worst results in our study! When you gesture you must do it like you mean it.

- Top middle and top right. How about doing no gestures at all? Again these got terrible results. Not quite as bad as limp gestures, but still very poor.

- Bottom left. If the only gesture you make during a speech is palms down, between waist and shoulder height, arms slightly away from your body, your ratings shoot upwards. You're seen as more inspiring and convincing.

- Bottom right. Similarly, if the only gesture you make is palms upwards, between waist and shoulder height, arms away from your body, your ratings increase.

The best results overall came from combining bottom left and bottom right, using both palms downwards and palms upwards, in a way that was congruent with the message (palms downwards for closed statements, palms upwards for open statements or questions). It's a bit like learning a forehand and backhand in order to play a game of tennis. Of course, there are different nuances of gesture, just as there are nuances of tennis stroke, but fundamentally knowing these two will serve you well.

So that's arms and legs sorted. There is one final piece of the movement puzzle that you can apply to your legs, arms or your whole body to create a clearer message and more engaging journey for your audience. This one is my favourite.

TIME TRAVEL

This is one of the most transformative tools I have come across for improving how you communicate with people. It creates greater clarity when you speak and increases your influence. It relates to how we visualise time.

Try these experiments

1 Draw a line across the middle of a piece of paper. Then write 'January' at one end of the line and 'December' at the other end, to create a timeline. Put it to one side.

2 Imagine you're talking to a friend. Use gestures as you tell the friend about what you did:

a) last week

b) this week

c) what you will do next week.

Notice which directions your hands move in, when you talk about the past, present and future.

3 Draw the letter 'M' with your finger, in the air.

If you're like most people, here is what happened. You wrote the word January on the left of the page and December on the right of the page. You gestured to your left for last week, in front of you for this week and to your right for next week. You drew the letter 'M' starting at the left and moving towards the right.

This is how most people see time. We believe the past is on our left, the present is in front of us and the future is on our right.

There are many theories about why this works. In most languages, reading and writing goes from left to right. Also, if you ask someone to talk about the past, most will move their eyes to the left (known as an 'eye-accessing-cue' that helps you retrieve a memory) and if you ask them about the future their eyes will move to the right. Left-handed people usually gesture in the opposite way (but as most people are right-handed, left to right has become the norm). And, perhaps surprisingly, no matter where in the world I am teaching, the timeline expectation holds true – even in cultures where the norm is to read and write from right to left.

In life, presenting something that you've worked on for a while beforehand will mean that your gestures will likely move from your left to your right, as you move through the timeline of events. That helps you map out what you're saying – but for the people sitting in front of you, it's the wrong direction.

In order to give your message greater clarity you need to flip around your gestures and make them work for your audience, gesturing to your right for the past and to your left for the future. If you're on a large stage or in a big meeting room and you want to walk in order to bring in everyone in the room, move to your right as you talk about the past and to your left to talk about the future. Your audience then gets a clear, visual timeline. Your words and actions match, reinforcing your message.

EXPANDING YOUR COMFORT ZONE

In coaching sessions our team often encourages people to 'go too far'. By this I mean gesturing bigger and speaking with more enthusiasm than we might expect in the workplace. Clients may report that they feel over the top, exaggerated and as if they're performing. Then we check with their colleagues and managers who are sat watching them. Most will tell them that they look great.

I experienced the feeling of being over the top when I attended a speechwriting workshop. Max Atkinson, who is sometimes called the UK's godfather of modern speechwriting, was taking the course. Professional writers have been devouring his book, *Our Masters' Voices*, for decades. The final task of the day was to write a short speech using all the techniques he had shared. 'Go for it,' said Max. 'Use every tool far too much, beyond what you think you should do.' This advice sounded familiar, so I went for it.

Then, I stood up to deliver my speech to the group. I felt bad, because, by applying the techniques in every sentence, it sounded as though I was poking fun at them. When I finished there was a short silence. 'That was fantastic,' said Max. I thought he was kidding! The group agreed. 'Genuinely, you should do it like that, even if it feels weird. It sounded good to us.'

I doubted this was true, so I put it to the test. I developed the speech into a much longer version and delivered it in Rotterdam to an audience of 900 students and business leaders. They seemed gripped, applauding and laughing in all the right places. So I submitted it as a competition entry for the Cicero Award, hoping to gain professional feedback. This contest usually has hundreds of entrants from professional speechwriters who work across Europe, North America and Australia and is judged by a panel of experts based in Washington, D.C.

A few weeks later Twitter was ablaze with congratulations and my phone started ringing. I had won the worldwide competition and was given the Grand Prize Award for 'Best Speechwriter of the Year'. I couldn't believe it. It was all because I resisted the temptation to hold back. I did something that felt too much at first, then worked on the techniques, got used to them and made them part of my style. I had found ways to connect with people even more deeply, giving them what they needed from me, speaking in the way that we are all born to speak and listen.

So even if the techniques I'm giving you feel strange at first, keep using and practising them. Drop old habits and come back to the freedom of movement that instinctively feels right.

Chapter 6
You were born to use your voice

In 1984 Ann Brennan wanted to become a politician. She was frustrated with the state of the country and decided to run for office. To succeed she would need to speak at a political gathering. This posed a major problem for Ann. She knew very little about politics and had never given a speech in her life.

Back then Max Atkinson, my speechwriting mentor, was a researcher who studied the speaking styles of politicians. He was asked to coach Ann for a documentary called *Claptrap*. His mission was to help her achieve outstanding results in just a few weeks.

They assembled a team of advisors and created a terrific speech. The night before the event, they had one last rehearsal. The following day she would speak to a live audience of hundreds of people, many of them politicians themselves. Ann rehearsed the words, but her voice was flat. The message was lifeless. They all felt it would fail. Weeks of preparation were about to go down the drain.

Just then the voice coach on their team, Cicely Berry, asked to do some extra work with Ann. She marked her script with arrows and highlights that showed her how to deliver it, with emphasis, energy and vocal variety. The next day Ann put it all into action.

In a four-minute speech she gained six bursts of laughter, ten rounds of applause and finished with a standing ovation. Her voice had transformed the words from a script into a powerful speech that enthused, entertained and elated the audience.

Our voice has tremendous potential. We can inspire, motivate and move people into action, if we know how to use it. After all, the chances are that you could email everything you want to say. If you're having a meeting, you're not there to just give people information. You must give the words more meaning than an email, through your body language – and your voice.

In the previous chapters, we focused on how you stand and move because you need to get this right before you can use your voice effectively. If your body isn't set up correctly, your voice will be a reflection of that – tense, tight and tired.

There are still some other challenges that can get in the way. Most children make crazy and weird whooping noises just for fun, as if their voices are dancing freely. By the time we reach adulthood, that joyful abandon in our vocal expression has, in many cases, become strangulated. The result is that our words lose their power.

I think there are several circumstances as a result of which we 'lose' our voice as we grow older. Not all of them may apply to you, but even if only one of them does, that's enough to have a negative impact on your delivery. I think the most common culprits are:

- Being teased, bullied or criticised when you spoke up about something you believed in.
- Working in an open plan office – where speaking loudly causes a distraction for those working quietly around you.
- Being interrupted by friends, family or co-workers who felt their voice was more important than yours.

I once worked with a Scottish man who was very tall and broad. When he stood up to speak I expected a commanding voice, but he merely whispered in a high-pitched mumble. We worked on his breathing, relaxing his jaw and lowering his pitch until his full sound came out. When he finally spoke with his complete, natural voice he looked worried. He explained that a manager had told him that he was too intimidating and so he had decided to hold back.

I asked for feedback from his team. They said that the opposite was true. When he held back his voice and spoke in a high pitch, they felt he was tense and disconnected from them. When he let his voice go, they found it much easier to listen to him. He had greater warmth and connection.

His manager may have been trying to help. There may have been other reasons for his feedback. Either way, when we overcame the block and he heard all the good things his team had to say, he nearly cried. We all have a strong emotional connection to our voice, so releasing it can create an outpouring of feeling.

Another of my clients spoke faster than I've ever known anyone speak. Speaking too quickly gives the impression that our words lack thought; slowing down comes across as more considered and thoughtful. Even though my client finally learned to pace herself during the workshop, she told me that in real life, she didn't think she could do it. She felt she had to rush her words in order to get them heard. Why? Because when she was growing up, her family had never let her finish a sentence!

As one final example, I recently worked with a young woman who said everything with a lack of effort and a shrug. Her tone was downbeat. I asked her why she might talk this way. After some thought, she realised that she had been teased when trying to get her point across to a group of students. She didn't want any sense of enthusiasm for her subject to lead to others mocking her. It took only fifteen minutes to coach her to talk again with power and conviction.

Of course, probably with a little bit of searching it will have been more than a single situation or event that in the end caused each of these clients to shackle their voice. But it's the single event that sticks.

No matter how great our ideas, everyone at some point says something that other people want to put down in one way or another. In order to release our voice, we have to be able to put single events into perspective. The truth is that the person who criticised, or interrupted or laughed at you probably forgot about it five minutes later. You have to let it go, too.

It's also worth noting that often when ideas hit resistance, in fact it's a good sign. Great ideas powerfully spoken create change. People sometimes fear change, which means it's often easier to try to stop it than to welcome and support it. Prepare yourself to hit resistance. And, when you do, respond empathetically and consultatively – and keep moving your ideas forward.

And there's another thing: we seem to be wired to remember the bad feedback more than the good. I wouldn't mind betting that for every criticism you've received about your voice or something you've had to say, you've also had plenty of positive responses. People may not verbalise their agreement – but if you suggest something and it happens, or people come with you, literally or metaphorically, that's positive feedback. Keep things in perspective.

Nonetheless, there are plenty of strategies you can use to bring your voice back to life. I think the three most important are tension, breathing, and the five Ps.

FREE YOUR TENSION

In order to function, our muscles need tension. However, years of poor posture, anxiety and stress can cause us to hold ourselves in ways that create muscle tension that, in turn, blocks our voice.

This isn't an instant thing. Tension can build up slowly over so many years that we don't even realise it's there. You may have heard the example of the frog in the saucepan. If you place a frog in a pan of hot water (I don't actually suggest you try this), it will immediately jump out. However, if you place a frog in a pan of cold water and gradually turn up the heat, the frog will boil (don't try that either). Frogs apparently don't feel gradual changes in temperature. The same is true of tension in our bodies – for many of us it goes unnoticed until it finally reaches crisis point.

Tension spreads

To demonstrate how significant the effects of tension are on your well-being, place your feet flat on the floor. It doesn't matter if you're sitting or standing, on a bus or at your desk.

- Put as much tension into your feet as you can, scrunching up your toes tightly, curling them up with as much tension as you can. Tighter! Scrunch your feet and toes tighter!

- Have you stopped breathing? Most people do. How strange is that?! I asked you to put tension into your feet, but the tension spread up your body and stopped your breathing.

The same is true with tension in any part of your body. It will spread. It limits the way you breathe, speak and move; you must release unnecessary tension in order to power your voice effectively.

The physical techniques in this section are intended for you to use before an important event. Focussing on simple physical actions helps to release stress in the body, calm the mind, free the voice and give us a sense of feeling present, or in the moment. Let's look at each area in turn.

Head and neck

Your head can weigh as much as a bowling ball. If it's not balanced properly on your neck you'll create tension and strain your voice. There are two ways in which we most commonly misplace our head.

- Push. Do you feel that your head is jutting forwards slightly? The muscles in your neck and shoulders will strain as they hold your head in this unnatural position. Imagine holding a bowling ball out in front of you. Your arms would get tired.

- Pull. Other people tuck in their chin towards their neck. This strains the muscles up the back of your neck and in your throat. It muffles your voice and creates a negative tone.

Release your head and neck

Try this to overcome both the push and the pull. Imagine a piece of thread going from your spine, up through your neck and the top of your head. Imagine someone holding this thread above your head and pulling your posture upright gently. Feel the placement of your head adjusting. This may feel awkward or unusual at first, but you're simply reminding your body how it used to hold your head, and reawakening the muscles in your head and neck to this position.

Jaw

There is no doubt that speaking with conviction takes courage. However, so many people get in their own way of being brave. They clamp their jaw shut tight to stop the sound coming out at all. The jaw is also commonly where we hold lots of stress – literally gritting our teeth to face the day.

Release your jaw

Try this. Start with a soft chewing motion to warm up your jaw muscles. Then place your hands on your face, just in front of your ears. Softly rub your jaw muscles downwards, to help release them further. Now, open and close your mouth, opening wider each time, until you have eased away all the tension and your jaw feels loose and relaxed. A loose and relaxed jaw is the only way to allow a full and natural voice to come out.

Face

I once taught a lady who refused to make any facial expressions as she spoke because she didn't want to get any wrinkles. I've also taught both men and women who don't want their faces to give away their emotions. After all, the workplace is no place for emotions, right?

An audience engages with and responds to the visual signals in our facial expressions. Research by Vilayanur Ramachandran shows that we have mirror neurons in our brain that help us to understand how other people are feeling. Watch a friend or family member as they watch a movie – you'll probably be able to see the emotions they're feeling along with the characters in the movie all over their face. They show fear if the characters are afraid, they smile when the characters are happy. That's mirror neurons at play.

There are an astonishing forty-three muscles in the human face. Together they allow us to express ourselves. Make use of them, even on the phone! People will hear your facial expressions in your voice.

Shoulders

When I first started giving presentations, I used to go home with aching arms and a tight back. I was holding my tension in my shoulders and I'm certain my audience could hear it in my voice.

Release your shoulders

Stand comfortably, with your arms loose by your sides. Grip your hands together behind your back. Lift your shoulders up to your ears, as high as you can. Now, release the tension, drop your shoulders and swing your arms freely, forwards and backwards. Your shoulders should settle lower and the muscles in your neck, shoulders and back should feel more free.

Stomach

Having 'butterflies in your belly' or knots in your stomach makes it harder to breathe. And, as we'll see, breath is essential for your voice. Tension in your stomach pushes your voice from the wrong place, straining it.

To release tension in your stomach, simply tense and release your stomach muscles. This doesn't mean collapsing your posture. Sit or stand upright, then tense your stomach muscles as tightly as you can. Then, holding your upright posture, release.

Legs, buttocks & feet

Remember the experiment you did earlier in the chapter? Tension in your legs, buttocks and feet can lead to breath-holding.

Release your lower body

Working downwards, consciously tense the muscles in your buttocks, thighs, knees, calves and toes as much as you can. Then, work back upwards, consciously releasing the tension as you go – release your toes (give them a wiggle), your calves, your knees, your thighs and finally your buttocks.

When you're in an important meeting, check your legs and feet from time to time. If you feel any tension, soften your knees to let the tension go.

LEARN TO BREATHE AGAIN

Our breath is inherently linked to our emotions. When we are surprised, we gasp; when we are sad or relieved, we sigh; when we are frightened or tense, we hold our breath. When we are relaxed, we breathe slowly and deeply.

I have been told by well-meaning friends and family to take a deep breath and everything will be fine. Sadly, as kind as the advice is, for most people, it doesn't quite work this way. Let me show you why.

Check your body for tension – how do your shoulders, neck and stomach feel? What about your face? Your legs? Now, take a deep breath in and hold it for as long as you can. Have your shoulders gone up? This is what happens for most people. When asked to take a deep breath most people actually take a high breath, breathing into the top of their lungs. This is called clavicular breathing. (You can breathe normally now!)

Doing this means that you are breathing on top of dead air. If you walk into a meeting without lovely fresh air in your lungs, you will likely feel out of breath quickly and need to take another snatch breath on top. I've seen some people do this again and again, until they feel like they may explode!

To feel calm you need to trigger diaphragmatic breathing. This is the natural way we were born to breathe and it causes the abdomen to rise and fall, rather than the upper chest (watch a sleeping baby breathing to instantly see what I mean). It is breathing deep into your lungs where there are more alveoli, the air sacs that process oxygen. Oxygen helps to burn off adrenaline (the stress hormone), and the less adrenaline you have circulating around your body, making your muscles and your mind twitchy, the more in control you will feel.

First, though, if you want to take a full deep in-breath, you must empty your lungs of dead air. Breathe out fully. Once you've done that, relax and let your natural breathing mechanism take over. Of course, you may have years of habitually shallow breathing to override, so you may need a bit of a kickstart. Try this (many athletes do it to prepare for a race or an event):

- Stand or sit upright, keeping your body fairly relaxed. Place hand on your stomach.

- Push all of the air out of your lungs making a 'shhhh' sound, squeezing your stomach gently inwards as you do so.

- Keep your body upright as you push out the air, until you have nothing left.

- Pause for two seconds, keeping your hand on your stomach, then relax and let the air come back in. Naturally, don't force it.

You should have noticed your hand moving outwards, as air came deeper into your lungs. Breathing this way will cause your diaphragm to widen and push downwards, which causes your belly to move outwards. If you didn't feel this, just try again. At the end, don't think about breathing in – just let the air stream into your body.

When you feel confident doing this you can go further to establish a rhythm of breathing that helps to lower your heart rate, oxygenate your body and calm your mind. Here's how to do it.

'5552' rhythmic breathing

I practise this before every important event. It's the final step in my preparation, moments before walking through the door or onto the stage. You can even do a silent version of it while sitting in a boardroom meeting waiting for your opportunity to speak.

- Push all of the air out of your lungs as you learned before, with your body upright, making a 'shhhh' sound. Pause for 2 seconds.

- Let the air come back in for a slow count of 5.

- Hold the air in for 5 seconds (this gives your body time to process the oxygen).

- Push the air out slowly for 5 seconds, then hold again for 2.

- Repeat the whole sequence: in for 5, hold for 5, out for 5, hold for 2.

A few years ago I faced one of my toughest challenges on stage, speaking to 1,000 people on a large round platform in the centre of the audience. There was no lectern, nowhere to hide, no place to keep notes. All of the speakers at the event were feeling nervous, so it

pick up on the collective tension. The event started at
eaking slot wasn't until 3pm. As my slot got closer, my
lding, so I focussed on my breathing. My preparation
my content was strong, now it was all about getting
ate. I went through the 5552 technique for the final
thirty minutes before my session.

When I got on stage, the technology had some glitches. The slides were not changing properly, so it was hard for me to know what the audience was seeing on the massive cinema-sized screens high above my head. I believe that I kept my composure, not because I'm a seasoned speaker, but because of the breathing I'd done before I set foot on the stage.

I encourage you to commit to this technique as I am sure it will bring you great results. Not only will it give you a sense of calm, but when you have released unnecessary tension from your body and allowed yourself to breathe fully, you will be able to use more range in your voice. And that means you will be both a more relaxed and a more engaging speaker.

USE THE 5 'P'S

Our voice is an incredible tool when it comes to helping us communicate feelings. If you take the words of a song and read them with no feeling, they have no impact. When singers bring those words to life, with phrasing, tone and harmony, people are compelled to listen and their emotions align to the song. If we can apply the same principles when we're talking, we can change the way people feel about and respond to our words. This is where the 5 Ps come in: Pitch, Pace, Pause, Projection and Passion.

Pitch

Your voice has a huge 'range'. If you use the notes and tones to the best effect, you can immediately communicate how your listeners should feel about what you're saying. You have only to watch the news to see this in action.

News presenters take the most important information from around the world and then tell us how to feel about it using their pitch. They often do very little with their bodies (most sit behind a desk). They rarely change their pace. Their main tool to convey the meaning of critical issues is the pitch they choose for each story.

If a newsreader speaks in a lower pitch, the issue is serious. In a higher pitch, the story is likely to be uplifting, positive or surprising. For example, try reading the following:

In a low pitch: 'Our main news today will be an update on the economy.'

In a high pitch: 'And we have information about the new royal baby.'

This should sound as if there is a problem with the economy, but there is great news about the baby. Now read the sentences again, but reverse the pitches. This time we think the economy is going well and there is bad news about the baby.

How we respond to pitch reflects how our voices change as we grow from children to adults. Children have higher voices, so we associate a high pitch with youth, excitement, energy, hope and free-flowing joy. As we get older, male or female, we gain a lower range. In which case, lower pitch conveys wisdom, authority, experience and, to a certain degree, seriousness.

ACTION!

Make sure you vary the pitch as you talk. We need variety in order to keep listeners engaged.

In order to loosen up your range, you can do what's called 'sirening'. It feels a bit like humming, but rather than using your lips and making the sound at the front of your mouth, you make the sound further back, to warm up your vocal chords and open your full range.

Sirening

I practise sirening before every major speech I give, to ensure I can use my full range without croaking or cracking. It takes only a few minutes. Make sure you have released tension from your body before der that you don't strain your throat.

'ng' sound, as in the sound you make at the end of the
'. Hold it.

ng the sound, slide up and down in your pitch, getting
higher, then lower, then higher, then lower.

- Use your hand to extend the range as much as you can: move it
up and down with your voice, to encourage your sound higher
and lower still. (As you reach the highest notes, your eyebrows
may go up, too!)

I highly recommend using arrows on your notes to help you
remember to use your full range when you speak. It may seem
unnecessary, but under pressure your throat may tighten up, making
using your range difficult, or you may simply forget in the stress of the
moment. Arrows on your notes can be incredibly effective at keeping
your focus and message alive. Just draw upwards arrows to remind
you to speak in a higher pitch for positive messages and downwards
arrows for moments when you need to sound serious.

Pace

Pitch and pace are like twins. If you put them together, they amplify
each other. And, in a similar way to pitch, a high pace creates a
sense of excitement; a low pace creates a greater sense of gravitas.
Composers use pace to the same effect when writing music.

Learning to pace your speech is really important. In the pressure
of the moment, fear can take hold. Your heart rate will increase and
that often means rushing through what you have to say in order to
finish as quickly as possible. Try saying the following.

At a fast pace, in a high pitch: 'I want to reassure you that we will
think seriously about everything you have said and will create a
thoughtful plan.'

Now try the same words with a slow pace and a low pitch. The
message changes significantly: in the first you sound like you're
panicking and don't know what you're doing. Your pitch and pace
make the listener nervous. In the second, you sound in control. We
feel confident and reassured about you.

Of course, it's also important to learn to switch pace. Sometimes, senior leaders think that their authority has to be matched in the gravitas of their tone. However, imagine saying this in a team meeting:

At a slow pace, in a low pitch: 'I'm really excited about the year ahead, so let's get out there and make amazing things happen.'

Then, try it high pitch and fast pace.

Serious or excitable? You need to decide which one is right for your message, to guide your audience on how to react. I recommend using the arrow technique again. Use a forwards arrow for fast pace, a backwards arrow for slow pace.

The most important thing to remember about pace is that when you slow down, its not about making the words longer. If you say each word slowly yooooou'll souuuuund craaaazy! Slowing down is really about putting longer gaps between the words. Space them out. Or in other words...

Pause

In our modern world silence is rare. Think about your average day. Perhaps an alarm clock wakes you; traffic noise and background chatter fill your commute; phones ring incessantly at work. If there is a single moment of silence, your brain thinks, 'What's happened?'

This is true of life in the wild too. A jungle is always buzzing with insect and animal noise. If silence falls, perhaps a predator is coming and the animals need to be on high alert.

If you have a critical message, write **pause** in your notes, use a highlighter pen, or better still leave a great big...

...blank space in your notes to remind you to pause.

When I was living with monks, I learned that they allow silence to be part of the conversation. They don't always reply immediately when the other person stops talking. They are happy to sit in thoughtful silence to contemplate what has been said, giving thoughtful respect to the speaker's words. While you can't always do this at work, you can do it before you make an important point. Pausing briefly indicates that what you are about to say is worth waiting for; it gives the message the space it deserves.

This works visually as well. If you take a dress and hang it on a rack with a hundred other dresses, people will expect to pay very little for it. Bargain shops hang their clothes this way all the time. However, if you take the same dress and hang it in a shop window surrounded by lots of space, the dress seems exclusive and buyers are generally prepared to pay more for it. Think of your words this way. Are they bargain basement deals, or high-value items? Your use of the pause will show people how much importance each message deserves.

Projection

Lots of people think projection means speaking loudly. In fact you can have excellent projection while whispering. When you speak to a group of people, you need to focus on speaking at the right energy for the room. It's not about volume, it's about intensity – supporting your voice from the right place, with the right amount of energy and conviction.

Being influenced by the intensity of the way someone speaks is human nature. The intensity sends a message of its importance. Let's think back to those tribal ancestors. How would you feel if one of your tribe went running past your hut at full pelt? You would assume that something important was happening. After all, why else would he expend so much energy when conserved energy might mean the difference between life and death?

If we hear somebody using intensity in their voice, the energy and conviction in their words convinces us that what they are saying is very important indeed. That's true whether what they're saying with intensity is spoken loudly or in a whisper.

Speak from your diaphragm

Never push your voice (it will make you hoarse, and unconvincing). Power your sound from your diaphragm and its supporting muscles.

- Stand up and place your hands above your hips, with your fingers in front of your body and your thumbs around the back.

- Imagine three giant candles about ten metres away from you. Make a 'tsss' sound aiming to blow out the imaginary candles.

- As you make the 'tsss' sound, you should feel a squeeze inwards, around your stomach area and in your back. This is where your projection should come from.

I remember pushing my voice many years ago. I had seen some great speakers who were talking to an audience of thousands of people. They would wait behind the stage as they were announced, with rock-star music and lights flashing as they entered. I thought this was how things were always done at a conference. Soon afterwards I gave a talk to 150 people in London. I decided to copy those other speakers, waiting behind the screen and running on to the stage as my name was announced. I spoke way too loudly for the room – a mere meeting room, not a stadium. I could see people leaning away in their seats, recoiling from the noise!

Afterwards, I went back to my acting-school notes on projection. We had studied Patsy Rodenburg's work on the 'three circles of communication', which she wrote about in her book *Presence*. This describes three levels of behaviour and energy that you use when you speak. 'First circle' is withdrawn, keeping to yourself, de-energised. 'Third circle' is too much, pushing your energy out towards people, in a dominant position. 'Second circle' is about connection, being energised enough to connect with those around you, no matter how big the audience may be.

A few weeks after I had blasted those 150 people practically out of their seats, I was back on stage at another conference for another company. I had the same material to deliver. This time, before the event started, I checked out the space and assessed the energy I'd need to deliver to feel connected with everyone. Then I sat at the back of the room to watch other speakers who went before me, noticing what kind of energy level was working best for the room.

When I walked on stage, first I looked at the back row and then at the front row, making sure I felt connected with everyone in the room.

Then I started to deliver my session. I got the energy just right – they laughed in the right places and at the end I received the first standing ovation I had ever had. I'd nailed that projection and connected with my audience in just the right way.

ACTION!

To get your power right, go to the room you'll be speaking in (or a similar space). Imagine candles at the other end of the room and use the 'tsss' exercise to feel how much energy you need to power your voice. Speak, using those same support muscles, imagining people listening at the back. If you strain, yawn to open your throat and release tension, then try again. Support your voice from deep in your body.

Keep in mind that a microphone doesn't change your need to project. If you speak with a weak voice, a microphone will simply put a thin sound through the speakers. You must still project your voice correctly to give it the energy required to connect with people. The audience, large or small, will appreciate it. And the sound technician will thank you for making their job easier!

SHOW YOUR PASSION

This section is quite different to everything we've covered so far. It's not about a physical skill, but a mental and emotional one.

I have worked with many clients who have told me that they are passionate, but I can't see it or hear it when they speak. They keep their passion hidden and thereby limit their potential. At first I thought that practising how to express themselves fully might be enough to help them overcome the passion-killing. Sometimes it works. But the bigger journey comes from the inside.

If you apply all of the techniques in this chapter, but you do so without true passion, then none of them will work. Speaking from a place of authenticity pulls everything together and amplifies your impact on your audience. However, you must be prepared to be vulnerable, to let people in, and to embody your feelings.

PUBLIC SPEAKING SINCERITY

STYLE

Children are passionate, raw and authentic all the time. My youngest son has requested that I play one special song over and over for almost a year now. Each time he hears it his face beams, his eyes widen and his passion shines through every cell of his body.

Naturalist and television presenter David Attenborough can make millions of people feel excited about the way an ant – or any creature – lives its life. His passion for the subject comes through so clearly in his voice that you cannot help but feel captivated. Chef Jamie Oliver does the same thing for food. US TV personality Oprah Winfrey became the great communicator we know her to be only when she dropped all the advice she'd been given about hiding herself and emulating others and instead set free her passion and spoke with her own voice.

Studies show that children freely express themselves until about the age of seven. Then self-consciousness kicks in. On top of that, they start to feel more judged – by teachers, peers and even those who love them most. Once we start working, harsh words from managers or colleagues can harden us further. Battleworn, many of the people I have coached over the years start to shut off. I want you to know that you can overcome whatever life has thrown at you to cause you to hide your passion. No matter how tough your life has been, nor what events you have lived through, you have it within you to freely express your passion, live your fullest life and express your fullest thoughts.

It may help to hear that I have been through this journey myself. In my darkest days following devastating events, I completely shut down from the people around me. Silently, I even considered ending my life. The idea of expressing myself passionately was absurd. I could barely lift my feet as I walked, let alone inject enthusiasm into my voice. Then a conversation with a friend changed everything. She knew that I was suffering and I would be missed if I were gone. I hadn't spoken a word of my feelings and I thought nobody had noticed my pain, yet she saw straight through me. It showed me two things. First, people care more about you than you realise. Second, there is no point in blocking out the world and putting up barriers, because someone – most people – will see through them. I dropped the armour, opened up and began to live with passion again.

I encourage you to do the same.

Tim Ferriss, best-selling author of *The 4-Hour Workweek*, described a similar journey. He went through difficult times as a child and thought that displaying emotion was a weakness. Later he realised that while his armour may have kept certain things out, it also trapped negative things inside. He stripped away his armour in order to live a fuller, more passionate life.

Here are a few things you can do to set your own passion free.

- If you're practising for an important presentation, try talking out loud about your favourite holiday, hobby or something else you're passionate about. Describe what you love most about it. Then switch to your work content and keep speaking with the same level of passion.

- Put on your favourite music, something that matches the mood you're aiming for in your meeting (inspirational? soothing? uplifting?) and practise talking while the music plays in the background. I find that movie soundtracks work especially well, but you might like to play something that brings back happy memories. When you speak at your meeting you'll remember how you felt when you practised with the music and it will help you to inject passion into your words.

- Think about your favourite actor. Who do you find mesmerising? Try practising a speech as if you're them. Don't worry about doing a good impression or accent! Just have fun with it. Think about how they would say these words if they were in a movie version of your meeting. Notice how much added energy you use when you speak with their attitude.

- Focus on your true passions. Sometimes you may need to talk passionately about subjects that you don't care about. You can inject passion into your voice the same way that I did when I worked at the Formula One team. I have no passion for motor racing. No interest at all. But I do love basketball. Whenever I spoke about cars, I thought about basketball. When I talked about drivers, I pictured Michael Jordan, the greatest basketball player of all time.

As Mother Teresa once said, 'All that is not given is lost.' So share your voice and passion with the world around you. By doing so perhaps you will inspire others to do the same. Let your armour go and let your voice come alive.

Chapter 7
You were born to adapt

As my company grew, we reached 1,000 event bookings a year. I was delivering around 150 of these, flying around the world to coach people from different cultures and industries. Occasionally, this meant teaching six days per week, with six dramatically diverse groups.

One week stands out. I had been teaching non-stop. It was Friday. We had been given terrific feedback all week from our clients, but this day started with an ominous message from one organiser: 'Half of the attendees have cancelled. The others have been told they must attend, although they don't want to be here. They all have deadlines, but I told them they have to come. So you'd better be good.'

I offered to postpone the event, so that we could teach them when they were under less pressure and in a better frame of mind. The organiser insisted on going ahead.

I stood up to start the event and put my usual skills into action. A room filled with annoyed-looking faces stared back at me. I promised to respect their time and give them plenty of value. A few of them sighed, some folded their arms, others looked at their laptops. As I began the first activity and asked them to stand up, there were groans and rolling eyes. I guessed that they needed a greater injection of passion and enthusiasm, so I worked harder and gave them my all. They looked more sceptical than ever.

About thirty minutes into the workshop, I was due to pass over to another trainer to deliver the next section. His style has always contrasted mine, which gives our clients a nice balance. He went up to the front, spoke with a softer energy, gentle movements and calm voice. They warmed to him. A couple of them smiled. They asked thoughtful questions. He seemed to be working less, but he was achieving more.

I sat back to reflect on what had happened. He was delivering content that I had designed and that I delivered myself the day before to a group who were highly engaged and complimentary at the end. Now I was failing to connect with these people and he was up there saving us both.

It was a huge learning point for me. Even if you have a really compelling communication style, you can still get a negative reaction. You can speak to a group who appear to love everything you say, then say those exact same words to a different group and get a bad response. When this happens you might think there's something wrong with the audience. In fact, it's just that your style didn't match their needs.

The elements we have covered so far are the tools of what you need; they are like colours you can use to create any painting you choose. If you want to connect successfully with all types of people in a range of situations, you must adapt how you apply those colours and always be prepared to paint a unique picture. In other words, you need a range of communication styles that you can adapt to fit.

Incidentally, sportspeople do this all the time. A tennis player may win hundreds of matches, but then meet someone whom they cannot defeat. The only way the tennis player might get round the problem is to adapt his or her style to fit the new opponent.

There are many styles that you can speak in, but there are four that are most useful to master.

MOTIVATOR

You can use this style if you want to energise people, often in short bursts, to inject energy into specific sections of a meeting. Many people open their meetings with this style – and then tail off, leaving the audience feeling a bit deflated. So, it's also worth remembering that the motivator style is especially useful at the end, if you want people to spring into action. When I ask my clients to describe a classic motivational speaker, I often hear:

- fast pace

- high intensity

- choppy gestures

- strong voice

Whether this style comes naturally to you, or whether it feels like something you will need to practise, being a motivator is part of the way we are all born to communicate. After all, you can immediately recognise those traits as motivational. You're built to respond to them in a certain way. People around the world do all of these things when cheering on their favourite sports team.

Start looking out for moments when you slip into this style so that you can remember that part of yourself. One day you'll need that version of you in a meeting and it's handy to know how to access it!

Tony Robbins is possibly the best known motivational speaker in the world. He can turn on this style whenever he wants to – as well as the other three styles that we'll come to. Motivator, though, is simply his favourite place to be. As a result he can speak on stage at his events for sixteen hours a day and keep people enthralled by his words at 2am after no coffee breaks. At some of his events, he even gets people to walk over burning hot coals with bare feet. It's extraordinary. I've done it twice. That was the power of his delivery style – he motivated 10,000 people at the event I attended to leave the comfort of their chair, take off their shoes and socks, go outside and do something they thought was impossible.

The pace and intensity that he speaks with is extraordinary. I first went to see him with one of my clients. I was sitting in the middle of the arena waiting for Tony and I had about 5,000 people in front of me and 5,000 behind. I doubted how engaged I could be in such a vast space with so many people. Then he came on stage and within forty-five minutes the whole arena was jumping up and down, cheering as loudly as they could. It was astonishing. How could one person achieve this?

He had lots of loud music playing and large screens projecting his face across the audience, but that wasn't where his impact came from. Proof of this came when another speaker went on stage the next day and the audience's attention drifted. As I watched Tony's style, I realised he stood out in two ways. First, the amount of physical energy he puts into his movements, voice and gestures is extraordinary. Second, his pace is exceptional.

The average person speaks at around 140 to 150 words per minute. Tony's pace is way beyond this. He will often reach up to 240 words per minute. Four words per second. Before I walked across those hot coals, he had been speaking to us at rapid fire for about eight hours, without a meal or bathroom break. We were ready to do just about anything at that point. Having accomplished the fire-walk, we felt euphoric.

COMMANDER

Sometimes you may need to deliver a serious message, with authority and precision. Those situations need the commander.

You can tell when a person you know well is about to say something deadly serious, because they add weight and importance to what they're saying by:

- speaking slowly

- using pauses

- lowering their pitch

- making smooth, controlled movements

- using palms-down gestures

My team often teaches aspiring leaders. These people ask for coaching because they feel they lack gravitas and authority when they speak. While experience and competence are prerequisites for leadership, in order to be treated like a 'tribe leader', you also need to embody certain qualities, including speaking like one.

Barack Obama had a highly motivational style back in 2004,

long before his campaign to become President had begun. At the Democratic National Convention, in a speech that triggered support for his campaign, he spoke rapidly with great force, motivating the crowd into a standing ovation. By the time he gave his inauguration speech four years later, he had slowed down his style, lowered his pitch and used more palms down gestures. No longer the motivational candidate, he appeared very much to be the 'Commander in Chief'.

Remember that each of these styles is an authentic part of you. You will have your own way of embodying them. The key is to look out for moments when you notice yourself dipping into the style, then get familiar with this part of yourself so that you can recapture it when you're delivering a key message or hosting a serious meeting.

ENTERTAINER

Sometimes you need a speaker who is going to lighten the mood. This doesn't mean cracking jokes or trying to be funny, it's a general feeling, a lightness and freedom that gives others the space to laugh, relax and joke around with you if they wish.

Comedians use many different approaches to get people to laugh. Some are grumpy in their delivery, others shout and swear. Those approaches may work for them, but they may not work for you. Think of the entertainer as the classic courtroom jester. You can create this simply by:

- speaking with a high pitch
- using floppy gestures
- talking at a fast pace
- moving around more
- using exaggerated facial expressions

These traits suggest that you're not taking the moment too seriously and you're allowing others to have fun as well.

You may want to use this style when you're having lighthearted conversations with people, before the serious parts of your meeting begin. Or, you might want to lighten the mood when discussing a serious situation. I've seen great communicators try this style to express incredulity and amazement at the craziness of a certain idea. It allows people to laugh about it rather than feel disheartened.

This one can be hardest for some people to master, as they put up a wall, saying, 'The thing is... I'm just not funny.' Don't worry about that. All you need to do is soften up physically and vocally. If you don't, people may feel that you're too serious all the time, unable to relax and enjoy life or laugh at yourself on occasion. It also diminishes the value of the most serious things that you say. After all, if you're serious all of the time, how is anyone supposed to know when you say something really important?

You may notice yourself behaving in this style with the people you feel safest with – perhaps friends from school, or others you have known for a long time. Whenever you feel most loose and carefree, notice how people move, speak and behave. You're all non-verbally showing that nothing that's said is meant to be taken too seriously.

FACILITATOR

Facilitator is the opposite of commander. When I was aiming to win around that tricky client, I hoped the motivator style would rally the audience into action. But it didn't work. When my colleague stood up, he spoke in his natural facilitator mode and won them almost immediately. When a tough objection came up from the room, he stayed calm, in his style, listened, and within moments quietened the objector altogether.

Facilitator is less about talking and more about listening. So much time, thought and preparation is given to delivering your message that sometimes we forget that communication is two-way. Facilitator mode creates the opportunity for people to collaborate with you, in a communal sharing of ideas.

If you're leading a meeting or pitch, being a facilitator doesn't necessarily mean you sit down and let someone else take over. You can facilitate useful discussions as a thoughtful leader, drawing in the voices of different people around the room. We instinctively feel we have a facilitator in the room, when he or she:

- talks less

- uses a softer voice

- uses soft gestures

- tilts his or her head

- stands or sits off-centre

All of these signal that you're no longer taking full charge of the meeting. You have softened your position to give space to others.

The most well-known British chat show host to use this style was Michael Parkinson, who spent three decades of his career interviewing the most famous people in the world. He always gave lots of space and time for the guests to talk, allowing them to open up deeper conversations and reveal the most fascinating insights about their lives. (American chat shows often work differently, with the host keeping the conversation buoyant and playful, high-energy and fast-talking – more like an entertainer.)

The Dalai Lama speaks as a facilitator. He takes a pause for deep reflection, then speaks humbly and warmly. This invites us to think reflectively as we listen to him. He can also flip this style into entertainer, making people laugh with him easily, then he flips back to facilitator when he needs to. Malala Yousafzai has delivered compelling speeches and spoken on panels at conferences while in facilitator style, embodying humility, poise and peace.

MIXING AND MATCHING

A consummate speaker is able to read the room and the mood and switch styles, both to keep the audience engaged, and to get the results he or she needs. When you're mid-flow with your best motivator and you get a question from someone who strongly disagrees with you, should you just keep going? Perhaps instead it's time to switch to the facilitator: pause, change style and give your objector time to speak. Listen well, then respond kindly and collaboratively. They will appreciate your ability to switch your mindset from focussing on the goal of your talk to caring about their interests. Only once an objector is calm, can you switch back to the style more appropriate for the general mood of your talk. (We'll discuss more strategies needed for handling tough questions later.)

Oprah Winfrey convincingly uses all four communication styles. She can motivate and energise an audience, share commanding nuggets of wisdom, entertain with playful moments, and then facilitate a guest into sharing intimate stories. It requires practise to glide effortlessly between styles, but once you can do it, you will be able to connect with more people in a greater range of ways.

WHAT'S YOUR PREFERENCE?

Having read these four styles, you may have an idea about which of them is where your talents naturally lie. Remember: you're capable of all four, so don't get too comfy! While it's fine to have a style where you feel most confident and at ease, you must be able to shift or you will quickly lose people who need a different rapport with you.

The motivator style has always been my favourite. When I started my company I was only twenty-three. I was often booked to speak in front of audiences filled with people older than me. At one speech I recall looking around the room of 200 people and guessing that the average age of the audience was sixty years old. The Mayor of London was scheduled to give them a talk about his life's work, but had to pull out at the last minute. I happened to email the organisers that week offering my speaking services, so they booked me to replace him. The audience had a lifetime of wisdom. I couldn't match their experience or gravitas, so I offered them youth, enthusiasm and energy. Thankfully, they loved it and I was asked to speak at their events repeatedly for more than a decade.

The motivator style seemed to match what people expected from me early in my career. And most of the time, it was well received. But I soon learned that some groups engaged with me and others needed something else. I had to expand my repertoire of styles.

Proof of this need came when I met a Sales Director from Australia, who was interested in us training his team on the Gold Coast. I was especially keen to win this job, but the guy was so laid back. His voice sounded like a late-night radio host who would easily soothe you to sleep. I tried pitching to him in my usual style. I gave it all I had. He wasn't keen. We lost the deal. I felt I had been over-zealous. A year later, though, he got back in touch. He had tried using a couple of other companies and was disappointed with the results. He wanted to discuss the options for working with us again.

We scheduled a call for 11pm London time, which was 8am for him in Sydney. My theory was that he would be at his perkiest while I would feel sleepier. I put on pyjamas, sat in my home office, leaned back in my chair, put my feet up on my desk and phoned him. When I spoke I moved my arms smoothly, as if conducting a lullaby, to soften and slow down my style. Later that day he emailed me to say, 'It sounds like you really understand us. We'd love to work with you.'

Have a think about which style you use most often. Then see how many times you can play with the other styles this week, so that they become easy for you to slip into – no pyjamas required!

STRENGTHENING YOUR SPEAKER SPECTRUM

Use the following questions to help you identify what style you most think suits you, which styles might need a bit of work, and how you can use all styles to become a more convincing speaker.

What style do you think you use most often? Motivator, Commander, Entertainer or Facilitator?

Which style do you struggle most to embody? (Quick tip: this will usually be the style that is most different to your favourite. Motivator and Facilitator are opposites, as are Commander and Entertainer.)

In what situations do you find it easiest to become each style?
Motivator?

Commander?

_____

_____

_____

_____

Entertainer?

_____

_____

_____

_____

Facilitator?

_____

_____

_____

_____

When can you try out each of these styles in the future? What events, what messages, what parts of a meeting will you use to put these styles into practice? (Remember to get familiar with speaking in each style, practising in relaxed situations before you go high pressure.)

Motivator?

Commander?

Entertainer?

Facilitator?

Chapter 8
You were born to lead

The most stunning finding in our research was that communicating the way you were born to speak could not only improve your daily life, but also change election results, the destiny of a nation and therefore world events. It's well known that during the Nixon vs Kennedy debate people who listened on the radio said they felt Nixon had won, whereas people who watched the television felt Kennedy was the clear winner. Watching a person debating critical issues under pressure is significantly more revealing than listening or reading a transcript. The person who makes the best visual impact has a strong shot at increasing their support from voters.

While there are many other factors that influence an election result, exploring the impact of communication styles on five leadership elections, on both sides of the Atlantic offers many insights.

USA 2008

In September 2007 I was asked to go live on radio in Washington, D.C. to give my opinion about who would become the next President of the USA. I was surprised to get the call as I live near London and at the time I knew virtually nothing about politics. Most of my work was focussed on body language, so I was unsure how we could cover this on the radio.

The producer assured me that we would put videos of the candidates we talked about up on the radio's website, so that listeners could take a look. We wouldn't be discussing political views, just their communication styles. I naïvely agreed to the interview, knowing that election campaigns in the UK are usually six weeks long, with a couple of major contenders. Little did I realise at the time how different things were in the USA. My radio interview was fourteen months before the election took place and there were seventy-three contenders.

I started to look through footage of the debates, speeches and interviews to find interesting styles to talk about. The first person I analysed was Rudy Giuliani. At the time he was the lead contender for the Republicans, with 21 percent of the support. Giuliani was an experienced speaker and used to being in the public eye, so I expected he would have a competent style. However, he had one habit that kept on cropping up, which I felt could work against him.

When Giuliani was asked difficult questions, he would pull backwards, away from the interviewer or lectern, pull down his chin in a protective position, clasp his hands low down in front of him and then respond. This is called the 'denial' position, where you're physically denying yourself the ability to be expressive. In this position you can't gesture, as you're restraining your hands, and your voice sounds muted or negative in tone as pulling down you're chin crushes your vocal channel. I felt this looked and appeared defensive, displaying a possible lack of conviction and confidence in his policies. This may or may not have been true, but this is how his style came across.

As it happened, only eight weeks later Giuliani had gone from first place to last – he had dropped out of the competition. There are hundreds of reasons why this may have happened, but his communication style certainly wasn't working in his favour.

The second person I spoke about on the radio was Hillary Clinton. According to the Gallup poll she had 50 percent of the Democrats' support, giving her a thirty-point lead over John Edwards, who was in second place. Eighty-six percent of Democrats had said they would vote for Clinton if she got the party's nomination.

Having anything above a twenty-point lead is rare in Democratic races. Previous candidates with such a big lead at this stage of the campaign had eventually won the nomination.

I started to look through her videos. There was an unusual consistency when looking at the footage of her interviews, convention speeches and her campaign website. She frequently appeared to be leaning forwards, jutting out her chin, with her arms up, making tense gestures. She didn't use this style before or after the campaign, so my guess is that someone had coached her, and I believe whoever that was moved her in the wrong direction. She had adopted the 'bluff' position. You may see people doing it when they're trying to sell something. Instead of winning support, the style is likely to put people off. In Clinton's case, it gave an impression of forcefulness unusual in someone who is confident in their ideas and abilities.

Others use the bluff position when making conference calls. People jut their chins forward and gesture towards the call box, attempting to emphasise their point. This just results in a tense voice, which doesn't carry well on the phone. It is much better to stand your ground (or remain centred, if sitting down) so that you speak with a clear, supported and convincing voice.

As we all saw, Hillary Clinton gradually lost her lead and eventually ended in second place for the Democrats. Again, there may have been many other factors involved, but her style may have worked against her.

Lastly, on the radio show we talked about Barack Obama. He may seem like an obvious choice at this point. However, at the time he was trailing in the polls and was almost unknown outside of the USA. I wanted to talk about him because I felt the two main candidates had poor habits in their communication styles. I needed to contrast them with someone who had a terrific style, to show the listeners what this looked like. Obama embodied so many of the elements I describe in this book, communicating in the way that we are born to speak.

You may have strong views on politics and you may or may not agree with what Obama stood for, but if you put those thoughts aside I'm sure you'll agree that Obama was the best speaker.

He stood in a centred position and walked elegantly with great posture. He had a great range of gestures that were congruent to his words. His voice would adapt to match his message, going through a variety of styles and moods to connect with the audience and captivate their hearts and minds. Of all the candidates, I felt his style was the most effective. I didn't say he would be the next President, I merely explained why his style would be the most compelling and persuasive to watch. We all saw what happened next. Whatever people thought of his policies, he was able to captivate people's attention.

Points to remember

- Avoid pulling back from people, whether you're seated or standing. It looks defensive, especially when you're under pressure. Stand your ground.
- Avoid pushing forwards. It doesn't strengthen your message, it can seem too forceful or appear desperate.
- Represent your message visually and vocally in a way that will compel people to act, based on how you're born to communicate.

UK 2010

The first ever live televised election debates in the UK happened in May 2010. I was asked to go on BBC radio immediately after the first debate had finished to give my views.

There was a heated argument on the radio between representatives from the three major parties, Conservative, Labour and Liberal Democrat. They were all keen to say that their candidate did the best job at the debate and had the best policies. To break up their discussion, the interviewer turned to me for a report on the communication styles of the leaders.

I told them this was a visual debate to win swing voters. Some people will always vote for one party or another. The people in between were the important ones to think about, because they were open to influence.

Gordon Brown, who was the current Prime Minister, arguably had the most experience to lead the country. However, his communication style was very difficult to watch. He would continually make fists and bounce them up and down. He had developed a strange breathing habit, sucking a lot of air in with his mouth wide open, as if gasping. He seemed bullish and lacked warmth.

Some people suggested that this was just his style, so there was nothing he could do about it. I disagree. You only have to look at the speech Brown gave a few years later in support of Scotland staying within the UK to see his true style on display. He gave a terrific, rousing speech. His voice was impassioned, he made broad sweeping gestures. If he had spoken that way when campaigning to be Prime Minister, I believe he would have gained more support.

David Cameron was the clear favourite to win before the TV debate. He was ahead in the polls and the election was his for the taking. His performance at that first debate didn't live up to expectations, though. He held on to the lectern, with his chin in the air, leaning back slightly. This made him appear stand-offish and aloof. In fact, when Nick Clegg (the third contender) mentioned that Brown and Cameron had not given clear answers on how they would pay for their policies, both men simultaneously stepped back from their lecterns in an awkward retreat. Overall, Cameron seemed competent, but his style during the debate lacked charisma.

Nick Clegg, the leader of the Liberal Democrats, was the outsider. His party was trailing far below the other two in the polls. He was most likely given a place on the stage just to make the debate a bit more interesting, to avoid it being just a back and forth discussion between the two main party leaders.

Clegg had nothing to lose and everything to gain. His style was more relaxed, assured and warm. He stood centred, making strong gestures and speaking with a naturally powered voice. When an audience member asked a question, he responded by asking the camera crew to move so that he could see the lady speaking and answer her directly. After this Cameron and Brown both asked for cameras to be moved, sensing they had been out-done by Clegg's human request.

To me, Clegg's style was the strongest. When I said this on the radio, there was a huge outcry in the studio. The Labour and Conservative representatives said how ridiculous it was for me to suggest that he had any chance of winning support. I didn't say he would win the election, just that people would respond well to his style.

I gave an example about how this can affect an election by telling them about a lady I met on a flight to Cincinnati, three months after Obama had become US President. I asked how she felt about it and in her deep Southern accent, she said, 'I'm so glad Obama won, I did not like Hillary's pant suits.' I mentioned this on the radio as evidence that many people who vote don't understand politics or policies. They're watching debates to see who they connect with as the best leader to represent their nation on the global stage.

The next day most of the newspapers led with the story of 'Clegg-mania!' saying how tremendous his communication style had been. One poll, taken after the debate, showed that Clegg was more popular with the nation than Winston Churchill. I doubt this claim, but he had clearly made an impact. He continued to do well at the following debates.

At the election there was no clear winner. None of the parties had won enough votes to form a government. This was mainly because a huge surge of votes for Clegg's Liberal Democrats had caused an unexpected split in the results. The Conservatives asked Clegg to form a coalition government with them. For the first time in UK political history, the leader of the smaller party in a coalition was made Deputy Prime Minister.

Clegg had gone from the man Cameron described as a 'joke', to taking the second highest seat in the Government. I believe that Clegg's communication style had a large part to play.

Points to remember

- You're a visual representation of your message. If you appear aggressive or aloof, people will be less convinced by your content.

- Stay human, stay connected with the people you're speaking to. They will feel this intention and reward you for it.

- Having the most experience doesn't mean you'll gain the most support. Your ideas will not speak for themselves. You must bring them to life.

Meanwhile, back in the US, the competition had begun to find a Republican to face Obama in the Presidential election in 2012.

Mitt Romney emerged as the Republican's nominated candidate, a man whom many felt was poor at interviews. Obama was seen as the clear favourite going into the first debate.

Then Obama faltered. To give you some idea of how badly his performance was seen to be at that debate, the following day I was working with a lady from Chicago. She was a keen Obama supporter and she was sitting with her head in her hands, saying 'What has happened to my President?! Why was he so bad?'

Romney had given a surprisingly strong performance. His posture was lifted, his gestures commanding, and his answers punchy and concise. Obama, on the other hand, spent a lot of time looking at his lectern, rarely glancing at his opponent. He was seen standing off-centre, with one foot raised behind him. He spoke with little energy compared to his usual style. Polls that week showed that Obama had dropped ten points, from a clear lead to an unexpected dive below Romney. It was the only time at which he trailed behind Romney and the single biggest shift in support during the course of one week in the campaign.

Neither party's policies had changed. While there may have been a few other factors, the nation had seen the communication styles side by side and appeared to view Romney as the strongest.

There are many theories about why this happened. Some said Obama had lacked time to prepare. Others said he was jet-lagged. The *Guardian* newspaper proposed that Obama might have done it all on purpose, because this would be a 'turn-out election'. That means the election was close enough that it would come down to how many people actually turned out to vote on the day. If you think your candidate is clearly going to win, then you're not likely to take a day off work and drive across town to go and queue for hours to vote. Did Obama want to create more buzz? I doubt it, but it's a fun theory!

Obama himself later joked about the experience, saying, 'You may have noticed that I had a lot more energy in the second debate.

That's because I felt really well rested after the nice long nap I had at the first debate!'

The second debate did indeed see a stronger performance for Obama. It was a town-hall style setting, where candidates sit on barstools and then step forward, away from any lecterns, to speak directly to the audience and answer their questions. His stance was strong, he spoke with passion and, between questions, maintained a confident resting position with his hands, holding the microphone at a mid-height position near his belly button, just as professional television presenters do when they're not gesturing.

Romney appeared weaker. His feet were close together and between questions he would hold his microphone low down, below his belt. It gave him the impression of being deflated or too relaxed. It is also known as the 'flashing fig-leaf' position, because every time you lift your hands, you seem to be flashing your groin!

The polls after the debate reflected the communication styles, showing that Obama was back in the lead. He went on to win the election comfortably.

Points to remember

- You must find enough time to prepare for critical events. Don't wing it, even if you're an experienced speaker.
- When standing without a lectern, rest your hands together, above your belt, so that they are in a 'ready position' from where you can easily gesture and look poised for action.

UK 2015

Next up came the 2015 UK elections, during which I did a series of interviews for the BBC. We discussed how the leaders performed after each of the live TV debates and finally did a post-election analysis.

This time things were much more heated, with up to seven parties represented on the stage at once. Out of these there are four people worth mentioning. Each stood out for different reasons.

Nicola Sturgeon, the leader of the Scottish National Party,

showed a strong stance, firm gestures and punchy statements. These, measured through a tally of laughs, cheering and applause, gained her the highest number of emotional reactions from the audience. She was the clear leader, gaining seventeen positive reactions in the space of one hour. Labour's leader Ed Miliband gained only three reactions. At the election, Sturgeon's party saw a huge surge in votes, winning almost every seat where they were competing with the Labour party. Once again, Sturgeon's style was closer to the way that we are born to speak, while Miliband lacked impact.

Nigel Farage, leader of the UK Independence Party (UKIP), caused quite a different reaction from the viewing public. His policies and messages focussed on how annoyed he felt with the current state of the country. He embodied this completely in his style. He would flap his hands up and down in exasperation, while bouncing on the spot, speaking with a frustrated tone and frowning face. His body language was a billboard for his campaign. Although he was unpopular with many viewers, those who agreed with him could have seen his manner as a physical representation of their own frustrations. At the election his party's support quadrupled from the previous vote.

Finally, it's important to look again at David Cameron. His style had changed since the previous election. His energy, stance and gestures were more commanding. His party gained an unexpected triumph at the polls. Again, there are many reasons why this happened, but I believe his style helped. The day the results were announced, one of my team was in a taxi on the way to the airport and asked her driver what he thought of the election. He told her that he didn't know anything about politics, but he had voted for Cameron. When she asked why he had chosen him rather than any other candidate he said, 'I just watched the debates and thought, he looks like a leader.'

Points to remember

- You don't need to meet people to give them information. You can email them your policies, ideas or pitch. If you speak to them face to face, you must use your voice and body to help represent your message.
- Be congruent with your words and actions.

This is the election that had journalists around the world asking why Donald Trump was gaining support and Hillary Clinton was losing it. They were dumbfounded to see Trump rise in the polls, especially given his shocking words, actions and scandals. At the same time, Clinton's campaign struggled to gain the support everyone had expected.

In a recent interview Clinton said that initially she couldn't understand why people felt that Trump won any of the debates with her. Then she watched one of them with the sound off. In their town-hall style debate, she thought Trump's answers were useless, but when she muted the volume, she saw things differently. She felt he dominated the space and she appeared too restrained.

Putting politics and allegations to one side, let's just look at the communication styles of the front runners in this race. In the Republican party, when Jeb Bush announced he was running for President he seemed like a natural choice, polling as high as 29 percent. Following in his father's and brother's footsteps, and as an elected Governor, he certainly had the experience for the job. But seemingly every time he went on television his ratings went down.

Before Trump announced that he would run for President, his rating among Republicans was 3 percent. When he launched his campaign this leapt up to 12 percent and seemingly every time he went on TV (which was a lot), his ratings went up again. Even so, a national poll taken in July 2015 showed that Clinton would take 59 percent of the vote and Trump would get only 34 percent (with the remainder going to third-party candidates). So what happened?

Trump's style, policies and words all matched up. They were all displays of dominance. His most common mode was to use a swiping palms-down movement. He would also point, wag his finger and make lots of thumbs-up gestures. When he smiled he would use only the bottom half of his face, while frowning in the top half. All of this appears congruent when matched with his campaign promises to build a wall, ban Muslims from entering the USA, and 'Make America Great Again'.

Some expected the 'Access Hollywood' recording, in which Trump can be heard bragging about assaulting women, would put an end to his campaign. For anyone else that may have been the case, but the fact that Trump had said these things didn't take anyone by surprise. Few people who were supporting Trump at that stage were shaken off. Had he campaigned on equality, peace and women's rights, things would have been different. Instead his style, policies, words and actions were congruent.

Jeb Bush was the opposite in his approach. His movements were soft, his voice was quiet and his gestures appeared awkward. My guess is that he was given advice to gesture more, but he hadn't been shown how to do it naturally. Many of his gestures began by him lifting up his shoulder and then moving his arm out.

Try it: lift both of your shoulders up towards your ears, put both arms out in front of you, turn the hands palms-up, then tilt your head to one side. How Presidential do you feel? This was a typical position for Bush during the campaign, which ended for him in February 2016, shortly after he did a speech that received so little reaction he said to the audience, 'Please clap.'

Bush may have had more experience and better ideas than other candidates, but his communication style didn't connect with people. If you can't rally support, your campaign will fail.

The main race for the Democratic nomination was between Bernie Sanders and Hillary Clinton. Sanders lasted far longer in the race than people expected. He spoke passionately and reporters said that he was lighting a fire under younger voters and encouraging them to take an interest in politics. One element of his style especially caught my attention.

While watching the second round of Democratic debates, I noticed an odd connection between Sanders' gestures and Clinton's. Several times they were seen doing the same gesture at the same exact moment, with one major variation. Sanders would be gesturing above his shoulders and Clinton's hands were always between her shoulders and waist.

Often, people who are accused of being too dramatic when

they speak gesture above their shoulders, which shows heightened emotions. You'll see this when someone gets really angry, or elated. If you place your elbows on the table during a meeting and then gesture, your hands will likely go above shoulder height too.

Clinton's style has evolved over the years. During this campaign I would describe it as mainly being one thing – controlled. She certainly had moments of passion, but as one chat show host commented, 'When you ask her a question, it's as if she is responding via satellite link, with an unusual delay to figure out how she wants to portray herself.' Of course, the situation put all the candidates under immense pressure. And Clinton wanted to choose her words carefully, in case they were taken out of context in the media the next day. But the disconnection made her seem too controlled, as if we weren't seeing the real person.

Clinton commented in a recent interview that she wished she could go back to the debates and be less controlled. She had felt rattled by Trump prowling around behind her and wanted to tell him – in front of everyone – to back off, but at the time she decided to be more restrained.

There is certainly a lot to be said in favour of keeping your cool and giving intelligent, thoughtful answers. It's also important to do so in a way that feels natural, dropping any armour that may get between you and your audience. Otherwise you can appear cold.

There are lots of theories on the factors that may have impacted that election, including sexism, racism and perhaps even Russian collusion. Despite all of this, Clinton looked back and commented that changes in her communication style could have made a difference.

HOW DOES ALL THIS RELATE TO YOU?

You may have had doubts about your own ability to lead. Perhaps you have looked at other people and felt they were born leaders and that you were not. Rubbish! We need as many good people as possible engaged in leading others, whether that's leading your team, community or country.

Our research shows that the same principles hold true

internationally. When we're looking for a tribe leader, or deciding whom to support, we subconsciously react to certain behaviours. We strongly prefer someone who is:

- Centred, not pushing their idea on us or retreating under pressure.

- Using natural and energised gestures.

- Taking up space, with feet shoulder-width apart for key moments.

Just in case you still think that these traits are unnecessary, remember that if you have an idea worth spreading, you need to stand up for it. It won't gain popularity just through sheer brilliance. Great ideas don't change the world until someone communicates them in a way that inspires people to act on them. You cannot just 'be yourself'. You must strip back subconscious habits to reveal the power you were born with.

I encourage you to speak out about your ideas. If you don't then someone else will put their ideas forward and they may not be as worthwhile as your own. Historians often mention that Adolf Hitler was a compelling orator. He might not have caused so much appalling devastation without his ability to command a stadium of followers. Winston Churchill once said that World War II was ultimately a battle of ideas and beliefs. His powerful speeches inspired a nation and helped power it towards victory.

The Oscar-winning movie *The King's Speech* is based on the true story of a royal leader, King George VI, who suffered with a stammer and hired a coach to overcome it. One character increases the intensity of the film by saying, 'If his speeches can't inspire people we'll lose the war.'

John F. Kennedy spoke with great passion about putting a man on the moon. If he had sounded uncertain, nervous or apathetic, he may not have motivated the thousands of people who were involved in making that vision a reality.

Malala Yousafzai was just seventeen years old when she won the Nobel Peace Prize, two years after the Taliban attempted to murder her. Not one to be silenced, she has given many tremendous speeches since then. The Taliban wanted her to be a victim, but she became a leader, using her recognition as a platform to campaign for women's rights to an education.

Great speakers and leaders are not born remarkably different from you. You have all the tools you need – a brain, a voice and a body. There are elections going on all the time where the more effective speaker wins (although that doesn't guarantee success in office, of course). This is also true for sales pitches, interviews and team discussions. You may have better ideas, but in this media age it's more important than ever that you know how to connect and communicate your message. There is no longer any way to hide behind excuses.

Step boldly forwards and stand up for your ideas. Be strong, speak up and let the world hear you. Your voice matters. Don't hold it back with old habits. Set it free.

PART 2
STORY

Chapter 9
You were born to tell stories

'What can I do for you?' she asked. I had spent every penny I owned on travelling to India, teaching the monks and then studying acting. I was living in London as a broke, out-of-work actor, waiting on tables to pay my rent. I had huge debts and no idea how to repay them. I needed a job.

I went to a recruitment agency seeking work. The woman I met there sat me down and asked what experience and qualifications I had. I listed my education and life experience, expecting she would suggest an exciting range of sales or marketing positions in thriving, world-class companies.

'Moving furniture. That's all we can give you.'

What? Surely she was just messing with me? I had gone to a good school, gained decent grades, travelled the world and studied performance at a prestigious London academy.

'Isn't there anything else?' I implored.

'Nope. Based on what you've told us that's the only thing you're qualified for.'

I was shell shocked. I walked out of her office and stood in the street for a while, staring at the bleak future ahead of me. Where had it all gone wrong? Sure, I could move furniture for a while, but I was pretty certain that it wouldn't help me to launch a career. All of my courageous efforts had led to a dead end.

I walked around with a hollow feeling in my stomach, sensing that all of my dreams and aspirations had evaporated and the solid ground of life experience beneath me had disappeared.

A few doors away I found my unexpected salvation: a hairdressing salon. As I sat in the chair, getting my hair cut, the stylist asked me the usual questions. How was my week going? What did I do? What was my story?

I told him my journey in great detail, from timid child to monastery teacher and actor. He enjoyed the ups and downs of the adventure, as I passionately explained my ongoing quest in communication skills.

'Hmm,' he said, 'you should really teach some of those skills you've learned to my junior hairdressers. They need to improve their impact on our clients. I'll give you a free haircut if you do it.'

I was amused, surprised and terrified at his suggestion. I was confident on stage with a script, but I was still highly anxious around people in regular situations. How on earth would I be able to teach their streetwise, larger-than-life trainees?

I smiled and said it was a great idea. Then I paid, left as quickly as possible and decided I would need to find a new hairdresser.

I could never go back. Teaching monks was one thing. This challenge felt much harder. I had no idea what I could possibly share about communication that might be of value to anyone, least of all outspoken, fashionable teenagers.

After a while I reassured myself by thinking that the hairdresser would most likely have forgotten all about it. When I eventually went back he said, 'Richard, great to see you again. Your haircut today will be free. Come back next week and teach my team.'

He had thrown down the gauntlet and there was no way out. I felt compelled to do it. I guess I could have found an excuse, but then I realised something. He had seen much greater potential in me than the recruiter had. Haircuts in London are expensive. I did the maths. He was offering me five times what I could earn moving furniture. All I had to do was stand up and teach something.

I showed up the following week and gave them the best session I possibly could about communication. At the end of the two-hour session they said, 'That was terrific. When can you come back and teach more? Same time next week?'

A few weeks later I got a phone call from the head of an engineering company. 'I just had my hair cut today. I hear you're a communication expert. Can you teach my team of forty people before they work on an exhibition?'

And so it went on. Recommendations, repeat bookings and referrals. Soon I had built a multi-million-pound business – and it started with a free haircut and a story.

A recruitment expert had described me as almost unemployable. My hairdresser saw things differently. At the time this baffled me. Now it seems clear. I gave the recruiter a CV and a list. I gave my hairdresser a story. Same details, different delivery and my life was changed for ever.

Since then I have studied the science of storytelling, researched every different method I can find and created a simple yet powerful system that we have taught to thousands of clients. I'll be showing you how to apply this to every idea, concept or piece of complex data you need to communicate, so that you can bring them all to life and compel people to listen.

You'll be able to do this in all types of situation, including conversations, emails, phone calls, pitches, and speeches. It takes practice at first, but soon it will become automatic. After all, you were born to tell stories.

THE CHALLENGES OF BUSINESS STORYTELLING

You can't achieve much unless you have something worthwhile to talk about. However, even the most brilliant ideas can fail if they are described in a way that fails to captivate.

Whether you're talking in a meeting or writing an important speech, there are many challenges to face in order to turn your ideas into words. You may lack the time to prepare, have lots of dull data to explain or get stuck trying to make something complicated more concise and compelling. Some ideas die under a crushing pile of slides and graphs. Others get lost in jargon or waffle.

Imagine if you could spontaneously bring your ideas to life, hook your listeners right from the beginning, give them total clarity and leave them motivated to take action as soon as you finished talking. You can do all of this by returning to your natural instincts.

Some people assume that they know how stories work because they have heard plenty in their lifetime, but that doesn't guarantee success. You may have heard lots of music, but that doesn't make you a brilliant composer. By the end of this section, you'll know exactly how to tell effective stories that are memorable and motivate people to act on your ideas.

Storytelling has become a very popular subject to talk about in business today, with many people claiming that they do it – but few truly understand it. For example, I was at a conference recently that included a discussion about leadership. There was a panel of business leaders on stage and all of them mentioned how important storytelling was to inspire teams and improve marketing. However, none of them could give a clear description of what storytelling meant. When asked how exactly they were using stories, one said that their leaders tell people about their lives, including things they did while growing up and what they have done in their career. That's not a story, that's just a list.

When people don't understand the structure of a great story, they end up saying 'this happened, then that happened'. That's not a story. Stories require vital elements, in the right order to captivate the listener. Put simply, when it comes to storytelling most people tend to do lots of telling and not enough story. The types of story we're born to tell, remember and care about have to be compelling, because our survival used to depend on them.

As I was writing this book, I sat in the New York public library, in the main reading room, surrounded by an overwhelming wealth of wisdom. Every generation tries their best to pass on its knowledge to the next, so that humankind can thrive. For thousands of years before we had books, we had to do this without the use of a computer, not a piece of paper nor even an alphabet. If we wanted to save our children from the dangers of sabre-toothed tigers, we couldn't give a slide presentation and then hand out a leave-behind document for reference. We had to structure what we said in a way that would make sure our big ideas and crucial details would stick in the memory. Success in creating a compelling story was life or death, it had to tap into our evolutionary instincts, to ensure that our listeners understood and remembered every idea, every detail and every warning.

Most meetings today involve people telling each other information. Sometimes that information comes in the form of simple lists of facts. But, if you want people to take action, you need to motivate them. In the busy, noisy world that we live in, it is extremely hard to win and hold someone's attention. Lists do not capture the imagination and they do not inspire people to effect change. Read a child a basic list of events that happened to Cinderella and he or she will run off to play. Read the story of Cinderella, with all its textures, twists and turns and the child is gripped.

My children love stories. Reading them one (or five!) at bedtime is a favourite daily ritual. They ask me to make up stories on long car journeys, or while they're eating their tea. They think of stories as a treat, like candy for their imaginative minds.

Stories help us to make sense of the world. There are millions of data points around us every day. Stories give the statements meaning. When you speak in a meeting, rather than simply telling somebody what to do (which they can easily ignore), tell a story. This enables you to reach a deeper part of your listener's mind. Your story can plant an idea that transforms their behaviour.

Stories are especially important when you're talking about statistics. A number such as 3 percent could represent good news or bad news, depending upon the situation. The statistic is meaningless without its story – its context.

OUR FASCINATION WITH SOCIAL MEDIA

How many times have you been at dinner with a close group of friends and noticed some of them checking their phone for messages, or going on social media? People even think it's acceptable to do this during business meetings.

Why is social media so compelling? Because every Tweet, every Facebook post, every Instagram or Snapchat caption is a little story about someone else's life. Social media tells our own story on a daily basis, and the stories of others. Time and attention are valuable commodities. Social media has figured out how to earn both of them. Your stories must do the same.

Prolific author and marketing teacher Seth Godin wrote, 'It's entirely possible that people aren't listening closely to you anymore. There's so much noise, so much clutter... hoping that customers, prospects, vendors and co-workers will stop what they're doing and listen carefully enough to figure out what you mean is a recipe for frustration. Rather than insisting that people listen more closely... speak more clearly.'

This chapter will show you how to:

- Deliver a powerful speech or pitch, with a storytelling structure that's easy for you to remember and engaging for your audience.
- Instantly explain your ideas in a meeting in a concise and compelling way (and so that you're never stuck for words when your boss asks your opinion).
- Write persuasive emails and documents.
- Make your products and ideas more meaningful.
- Transform the way your team or company communicates, saving time and bringing clarity to every important message you share.

THE RESULTS CAN BE IMMEDIATE...

I once worked with a business owner who had been rejected by every investor he had pitched his business to. He then attended a half-day seminar with me and left feeling determined to try again. I met him a few months later when he returned to do a longer workshop. I asked how he was getting on and he said, 'I had to come and work with you again, you made me £500,000!' He explained that he'd gone back to the same investors, with the same numbers and ideas, but he had re-structured his pitch using the story system. One of them agreed to give him £100,000 per year for five years to help his business grow.

The facts he shared were the same, but he delivered the content as a story, enabling his investors to quickly see the value in his business.

When a lady at one workshop went rushing out as soon as we'd finished describing the story system, I was confused. About thirty minutes later she came back looking delighted: 'I nailed it!' she said. She'd spent the last half hour using our techniques for a weekly conference call with her team. That same team had spent the previous six weeks disagreeing with her idea on how to move forward with a certain project. In thirty minutes she'd written the story for her idea, had the call, told the story and finally won her team round.

GOOD STORYTELLING IS NOT ABOUT YOU

When I was first asked to teach clients about how to make their content more compelling, I decided to investigate what was going wrong. Why were good ideas failing to win attention? Why were people losing interest when my clients were delivering important messages in an engaging style?

I noticed that the problems seemed to begin the moment a person started preparing for a meeting. Clients told me that they would begin by thinking 'What do I want to say?' But that's the wrong focus. Why? Because nobody cares about what you want to say!

What people care about is **what they need to hear**. Your focus should be **the order in which they need to hear it**, in order to be hooked at the start, compelled to listen throughout and motivated to take action at the end. The next time you begin sharing important information, this is where you need to start.

Lack of time to prepare and distilling complex or dry information into clear, understandable and engaging form were also problems I needed to address. I wondered if there was a way to fix everything.

I searched everywhere to find a solution that would work for all our clients, across industries, cultures and continents. I wanted a concise, compelling and memorable system that any client could use quickly in any situation. It had to minimise preparation time, but still maximise the effects and allow key ideas that would compel listeners to engage from beginning to end, to stand out.

THE FOUNDATION OF EFFECTIVE STORYTELLING

I looked through countless books and research and noticed that many of the best storytelling methods were based on the 'hero's journey'.

Joseph Campbell, author of *The Hero with a Thousand Faces*, was the first person to describe this in detail. He studied many different kinds of story, including ancient myths, religious narratives and modern fiction, looking for the most powerful common elements between the various types. He realised that more than 3,000 years ago, ancient storytellers were using the same key devices that successful modern storytellers use today.

The *Epic of Gilgamesh* is considered one of the earliest known works of great literature. An epic poem, it was chipped into clay tablets and is believed to have been written by many different people, who added to the narrative over the period of a millennium. Joseph Campbell noticed that, despite the fact that William Shakespeare could never have read the poem (it wasn't discovered until the 1900s), Shakespeare used many of the same storytelling techniques in his plays. More recently, great Hollywood epics – from *Star Wars* to *The Lion King* – have used the hero's journey. Campbell explains that people across time and around the world are telling the same story over and over again. Whether Gilgamesh, Romeo, Luke Skywalker or Simba, they're just changing the hero.

Robert McKee is often described as Hollywood's godfather of screenwriting. His students have, between them, won sixty Academy Awards and two-hundred Emmys as a result of their skill in storytelling. He states that there's no such thing as a magic formula for a story, but there is a **form** – a structure with clear elements that the audience expects to discover and that allows them to travel the story's journey with the storyteller.

HOW CAN THIS WORK FOR YOU?

I know that no one presenting a medical paper intended to save patients' lives, or a quarterly board report intended to reassure shareholders is going to want to start their story 'Once upon a time...'. Yet, I also agree with Nobel Prize winner Daniel Kahneman, who once said, 'Nobody ever made a decision because of a number. They need a story.' But can storytelling really work in a data-driven, high-powered, professional environment? I was determined to come up with storytelling techniques that my clients could apply universally, in every culture, every environment, every situation and every medium. So I created a model that would work equally well in face-to-face meetings, delegation speeches, and intimate conversations, as well as in emails, conference calls and written documents.

This storytelling structure engages both the logical and emotional parts of the brain, ensuring that people get the data they need, as well as feeling more emotionally compelled to act on your ideas.

FIRST THINGS FIRST: YOU ARE NOT THE HERO!

Your role is the mentor. There are two key figures you often meet early on in a story – the hero and the mentor. The hero is the person who goes on a journey (usually from difficulty and pain and through challenges) to create a better future. The mentor is the hero's guide on that journey. In *Star Wars* the hero is Luke Skywalker; the Mentor is Obi Wan Kenobi. In *The King's Speech*, the hero is the King and the mentor is the voice coach. In Martin Luther King Jr.'s 'I have a dream' speech, the hero was the audience and the mentor was Martin Luther King Jr. himself. The same could be said of John F. Kennedy: in the speech in which he said, 'Ask not what your country can do for you, ask what you can do for your country', the hero was the entire US population, the mentor was JFK.

I've delivered events when the loudest cheers are definitely not for me. I am the mentor. The hero is the audience. When a volunteer gets up on the stage with me, follows my lead and tries out my techniques in front of everyone else, he or she is bravely taking the hero's journey for them all. His or her reward is always roaring applause.

Your company, products or ideas are not the heroes of your story. You may want to show everyone how great you are, but no one wants to hear you bragging. Your story must ignite a passion in your listeners (the true heroes), giving them belief that they can achieve great things with you as their guide (their mentor).

So, back to that regular meeting. If you're presenting a quarterly update, you're sharing insights that will help the boardroom executives (the heroes) on their journey to make good decisions about the company's future. If you're explaining a scientific patient case study, you're helping other doctors (the heroes) on their quest to effectively treat their patients. And so on.

ACTION!

Always be the mentor (the guide). Show the path, lead your heroes (your audience) along it and tell a story that will enable them to craft a better future.

Now that your role's clear, let's look at how to structure a great story.

STEP ONE – FIND PAIN AND PLEASURE

In order to engage everyone, from all backgrounds, you have to tap into our shared evolutionary instincts. The two universal forces that guide human behaviour are pain and pleasure. More specifically we are born to avoid pain and to seek pleasure. And, big or small, in every issue we face we're trying to run from pain and towards pleasure. Let's see how this works, at work.

Let's say that you're frustrated that the parking at your work is really difficult, and that finding a space wastes large amounts of your time and means you arrive at your desk frustrated and cross. You want to tell your manager all about it in a meeting. One approach would be to say: 'I have a problem. When I come to work there is nowhere for me to park. I have to drive across the road and leave my car at the railway station, then walk to the office in the cold and rain. This wastes the first thirty minutes of my day.' The focus is entirely the speaker. It sounds like moaning. Let's instead turn the audience into the hero – show them the pain and guide them on a path to make it better.

This time: 'We're facing a huge challenge. We're losing staff every month and when they leave they're taking our clients with them. The people who are left here do not feel valued, so we risk losing them as well. Our recent staff engagement survey showed that people are frustrated because there is nowhere for them to park. They start each day by being reminded of how little we are investing in them when they see that all our directors have reserved spaces, but they don't. We have 100 people working in this building and every day we lose the first thirty minutes of their time over car parking. That's 3,000 minutes per day of productivity lost, plus a demotivated workforce. What if we could fix all of this for virtually no cost, help the staff feel more valued and retain more brilliant team members and clients?'

In this version, the audience understands the pain, cares about it, and wants to avoid it. They learn about how they can remove the pain and turn it into pleasure: happier staff and retained – perhaps even new – clients.

What about a meeting that is all about numbers' update? You must give context, purpose and meaning to your data, so that people understand why they should care. What impact do your numbers, facts or ideas have on them? You need to give the bigger picture before you fill in the details.

Whatever your content may be, it is important to create a journey, showing how your information will help your hero move away from challenges in the past, towards a better future. To help further, it's worth understanding three compelling ways to enhance pain and pleasure in your story.

M.T.V.

All businesses care about Money and Time. They need to make money and be productive. People care about these too, but we also care about Values. We want to feel proud of our work, feel appreciated, have personal freedom, spend time with family, and so on.

Before you create any business story, think about your audience. What are the current challenges, pains and problems they are having in the areas of money, time and values? If you show that you understand these issues and you can show how your ideas will help people resolve them, they will be hooked.

Describing the problem in context

I hear a lot of businesspeople confidently describe the problems their audience members are facing. All well and good. However, things go wrong when they go from that to immediately describing their solution for making that vision a reality. In effect, they're saying, 'Here's a problem... here's my solution.' All problems have many possible solutions. Your job isn't to sell your solution. Your job is to sell the future. You must explain how your update, product or idea will help people achieve a more pleasurable or successful existence. Paint a new reality or remind people of the grander vision that they're working towards and how great it will be when they get there.

That's what commercials do all the time. They show a terrible, mundane world where a person like you is fed up with their life. Then they transport you to a wonderful world, where everyone and everything is fabulous... and reveal the product that will give you this marvellous life. If they started the advert by saying, 'Here's our product. This is what it does,' you would switch off straightaway. Instead they start with the bigger picture, painted in the colours of pain and pleasure, then they reveal the solution.

I've watched countless people show all of their spreadsheets and graphs before they mention how their data will help us. They'll end with a summary saying, '... and the benefit of doing all of this is X'. No! Start by telling me why your data is valuable if you want me to pay attention and listen to it.

As a business example of this, we were once coaching a company who were bidding for a £40 million engineering project. They asked us to watch their rehearsal of the final presentation. They were competing against three other companies so they needed to stand out. They talked through how they would deliver the project with all kinds of details on the engineering techniques required to complete it. After about twenty minutes I asked them to stop.

'How much of your engineering solution will be similar to the way that the other companies approach this project?' I asked.

'All of it,' they told me.

'So how can you stand out from them?' I asked.

'We're better at what we do,' they assured me.

'Great,' I said. 'Then say that at the beginning, otherwise no one is going to listen. Describe a better future that you will create for them.'

People tend to make up their minds very early on in a pitch about whether they will buy from you or not. Then they spend the rest of the time looking for logical reasons that back up their decision. That's why you have to win them early on.

We re-wrote the pitch as a story about the project, explaining the challenges the potential client would need to overcome, the benefits the engineering solution would bring and what the end result would be like. It was far more compelling to listen to. They won the pitch. (Of course, the presentation was only part of the decision-making process, but it was an important part.)

As another example, I once ran an event at which forty people from marketing agencies from around the world came to compete against each other for a large contract from a well-known client. They spoke to the client to find out what the project was all about, then they had just twenty-four hours to put their entire pitch together, working in teams from different countries. Every team came up with interesting concepts and shared professional strategies for how they would deliver the project. One group asked for extra coaching late at night to get their pitch to stand out. We worked especially hard on the pain-versus-pleasure piece at the start. 'Sell them an amazing future,' I told them, 'then show them how you will deliver it.'

On the day of the pitch everyone did well, but this team nailed it. They created a very clear picture about how the current situation was causing challenges for the client. Then they described a terrific, believable and exciting future. Before they even explained how they would achieve it, I looked across at the client and saw the smile on his face. He was sold. The team won with a unanimous vote.

Steve Jobs pitched Apple products to the world using his own version of the hero's journey. He would continually show people how they were currently in a state of pain, then create the allure of a better world and explain how we could all experience that future if we bought Apple's inventions. When he launched the iPod, he empathised with the pain music lovers were feeling – those who had to find space for hundreds of CDs and vinyl discs in their home. Plus, if you wanted to buy one song you had to buy the entire album. CDs were big and yet they would only hold about ten songs. He sold a better future. 'What if you could buy any song from any album for just seventy-nine cents?... What if you could have 1,000 songs sitting in your pocket?' You can, he told us, by buying an iPod.

The strange thing about this is that the iPod wasn't the first digital music player on the market. There were many available. The Sony device arguably had better sound quality. Others were cheaper too. But along came Jobs with his pain-and-pleasure intro and changed the way we listen to music for ever.

I didn't see the product launch. I was vaguely aware of digital music players, but I didn't understand how they worked. I quite liked CDs. I couldn't see the point in changing, until one of my clients told me a story. We were discussing music and I mentioned my favourite CD. He recoiled, saying, 'You don't have an iPod?!' It was 2005. I was a little behind the times.

'No,' I told him. 'I've got loads of CDs. Why change?'

He gave me his best sales pitch. 'After you finish working with us today, I bet you have a long drive home. If you want to change CDs while driving, you'll have to stop the car or risk crashing on the motorway. You'll be completely stressed out by the time you get home, mumble a few words to your wife, before collapsing into bed. Imagine this: if you had an iPod you could plug it into your car stereo and switch on your favourite playlist called "Drive it like you stole it!" You'll feel thrilled and stimulated the whole way. When you arrive home, you plug your iPod into the stereo with a romantic playlist and have the best night ever.'

I'm not making this up. That's actually what he said! He won me hook, line and sinker. I would no longer dread hours of driving and arrive home irritable and exhausted. Thanks to the iPod I was going to feel like James Bond. I told my wife the story when I got home. She bought me one straightaway.

Apple used the same kind of strategy to launch each of their subsequent products, including the iPhone. Jobs explained that smart phones were hard to use. Standard phones were not smart. What if you could have a beautiful phone that was really smart and easy to use? The iPhone was the solution.

Using this method at each major product launch helped Apple to become the most profitable company in history. Yes, they had beautiful products and great business strategies, but importantly they knew how to compel us to listen and then buy from them, through using pain and pleasure.

ACTION!

Think about a situation you want to change. Articulate the pain, then sell the pleasure of the perfect ending. Only after that, explain what people need to do to reach it.

Prime the brain to listen

Dr John Medina, author of *Brain Rules*, gives further evidence for the value of starting your story with pain and pleasure. He explains that when you experience a highly charged emotional event, your brain triggers the release of dopamine (the feel-good hormone). This is a useful survival tool, because when something makes you feel good, you are more likely to remember it and want to repeat it. You become better equipped to avoid pain and gain pleasure in the future. If you can tell a story that makes your listeners feel good, they will be primed and ready to hear your details and remember more of what you say.

Pain and pleasure in political storytelling

To explain the extraordinary power of pain-and-pleasure storytelling let's look at stories that have had a huge impact on millions of people over the past few years. Remember how physical movement can help politicians win votes? What about their storytelling ability?

There has been a lot of media coverage on Donald Trump in recent years. Some like him, others strongly don't. When it comes to storytelling, there is a valuable lesson we can learn from his election.

Can you remember Hillary Clinton's slogan when she raced for the Presidency in 2016? No? Nor can most people. It was 'Stronger Together'. Why is this so forgettable? It is just a statement of fact. Yes, people are stronger together. And the shortest distance between two points is a straight line. Neither of these facts is emotive enough to make you feel compelled to book time off work, get childcare arranged, put life on hold, drive across town and wait in line for four hours in order to vote.

Contrast this with Donald Trump. Do you remember his slogan? Of course you do: 'Make America Great Again'. Some of the media called it a joke. They said it was crazy that Trump couldn't point back to a specific time when things were 'great' in America, to give some sense of the golden era he was aiming for. There seemed to be little logic to his slogan. Nevertheless, it is very memorable and emotive, and has extraordinary influence. Why does it work so well?

'Make America Great' is a clear promise of a better future, implying that every American will be better off by voting for Trump. This moves you towards pleasure. The last word of the slogan is the genius element: 'Again'. This implies that America isn't great at the moment. Right now things are terrible. You're suffering. Things aren't working. The politicians don't understand you. You can't afford to pay your bills. The rest of the world is fleecing America, making bad deals that cause every American to suffer. But if you vote for Trump, he'll fix all that. He'll take away the pain of the past and give you a future filled with pleasure. That's the kind of promise that makes people feel compelled to get out of bed early and rush across town to claim the future they want at the voting booth. It may not be logical, but it's your emotional self that's compelling you to act.

In the UK we had a similarly divisive election on Brexit. The world was stunned when Britons voted to sever the country's union with Europe. So was most of the UK. Let's look at the storytelling.

The 'Remain' campaign pushed hard for us to stay in the EU. They had one message that basically said that if the UK votes to leave, it will be really bad. There was no mention about anything good that would happen if the UK remained in the EU. There was nothing compelling in the message, especially when polls showed that the UK voters probably wouldn't vote to leave the EU. The voting public had little motivation to show up at the polling station.

The 'Leave' story was much more emotive. It told voters that as a nation the UK is being controlled by idiots in Brussels, who take UK money and give the country nothing. Voters were told that leaving the EU would free up £350 million every week for the National Health Service. The day after the Leave vote succeeded, the leaders of the campaign were questioned about whether they would actually give that money to the health service. Of course they wouldn't! They didn't expect to win, so they made outlandish promises.

I'm not suggesting you make wild claims when you're trying to win a pitch. The point is that the Leave campaigners were very clear that the EU causes pain because it means we're powerless. They presented a more pleasurable future, with money being invested in something that would help every single person in the country.

Whatever you think of these election results, these politicians teach us valuable lessons about effective storytelling. Pain and pleasure principles can motivate millions of people to act. If you use pain and pleasure in your next pitch, presentation or election campaign, you have the power to create a new (and hopefully better) world.

STEP TWO – KEEP IT CONCISE

What is the classic problem when people share data and details in their meetings? There's too much of it. We can't remember it, we lose focus and switch off. It may be tempting to share all of your homework to impress us, but most of the time, it will leave us bewildered. Your story needs to create the vision of the better future, but not so that you overwhelm us.

US business researchers Iyengar and Lepper conducted an experiment aimed at finding out if we can have too much of a good thing (in this case, Godiva chocolates). Participants in one study group were asked to choose their favourite chocolate from thirty different flavours; another group had just six flavours to choose from. The group with thirty flavours started out feeling more excited and had greater anticipation of finding the perfect chocolate than the other group. However, at the end they reported they were less satisfied with their choice and less likely to choose the same flavour again. Those who had just six choices were much more satisfied.

The same researchers also conducted the Jam Experiment. They set up two stalls of different-flavoured jams. One stall had twenty four flavours, the other had only six. The stall with more flavours had 150 percent more visitors, but only 3 percent of them actually bought anything. The stall with six jams attracted fewer people, but 30 percent of them bought something. This meant that the stall with fewer data points sold four times the amount of jam!

So while it may seem important to show people every spreadsheet and piece of data you have, please resist! When deciding what to include, ask yourself this: what will your audience need to remember six months from now? Cut everything else out. If you feel the need you can always put the rest in a document for their reference. Just don't show it all at once.

Fairytale lessons in concise storytelling

Think back to the most popular fairytales you were told as a child. They differ from one country to the next, but most of them have one thing in common. The number three.

How many wishes did Aladdin get when he rubbed the magic lamp? How many bears did Goldilocks meet in the woods? How many ghosts did Scrooge meet? How many Musketeers are there? Three. We love things that come in threes.

You can see this in the way we talk about so many things. Past, Present, Future. Ready, Steady, Go. Have you ever stood at the side of a swimming pool and said, 'Hey everybody, let's all jump in on the count of four!' No! We expect things to come in threes.

Politicians have campaigned with three-word slogans. Obama said, 'Yes We Can'. Tony Blair said that he would focus on three things if he became Prime Minister, 'education, education, education'. Charities want us to 'Make Poverty History'. The supermarket giant Tesco promises low pricing, because 'Every Little Helps'.

What if you have twenty-eight things you need to say?

It is unlikely that every talk you'll ever give will conveniently fall into three main points. When you have lots of things to share, you can chunk them into three areas. Aim for three themes for your ideas, or three groups for your statistics. When Steve Jobs launched the iPhone, with its gazillion functions, he said, 'There are three main elements – it's a phone, a music player and an Internet communication device. Let me show you how each part works.'

You'll notice that this book has much more than just three pieces of information in it, so I have grouped it all into three major sections. They all start with 'St' – Style, Story and State. My aim is to make them more memorable for you, so that you can apply what you've learned even if you don't have the book close by (although I sincerely hope you'll sleep with this book by your side for years to come!).

Take a good look at your details and chunk them together into three themes or sections. That way people will feel more able to follow the journey and remember your key elements later.

Proof and process

Your pain-and-pleasure introduction will have already won people emotionally. Next you need to win them logically. You must explain the process of achieving your ideas, plus provide proof that your process will work. Graphs and charts, which I will cover in the next chapter, are both great ways of presenting proof and process information in your story in a visual and digestible way. Just ensure you divide your proof and process into no more than three sections.

STEP THREE – ACTION

Traditional storytelling tends to stop before we get the full picture of the future. The hero experiences pain, strives to achieve pleasure, goes through the three acts of the story, achieves his goal and that's it. When I was living in India, I was amazed to see that the local cinema even stopped playing the film at this point. They didn't let the credits roll, or show the final scene of people chatting about what happened and walking off into the sunset. They stopped the film when the good guy stopped the bad guy. People cheered. Story over.

But your story doesn't finish in the meeting. It has only just begun. In business things keep going. You can't just reach the end of the detail and say, 'That's it... any questions?' If they've listened to your story, they want to know what they should do to turn your ideas into action. They need to shift from knowing the path to walking the path.

Give clear forward instructions

First, don't make the mistake of asking for the world. Asking for a commitment of $10 million today is not going to convince anyone to give you the money. You will have wasted all your hard work. It's too big for the first step and people will opt instead for the safe option and stay put. Instead, give clear instructions that are simple to follow and start with an easy first step.

Rather than asking for large sums of cash, an easy step might be to agree to a date for a first project meeting. This is so unthreatening that your audience will happily start to move along the path with you.

Think of it like Harry Potter. If you said to Harry, 'All you need to do is go to wizard school for seven years, overcome the darkest evil in the universe, escape death countless times and stop the world from destruction,' he might have stayed hidden in a cupboard under the stairs. In the story all he needed to do was get on a train to Hogwarts. Once the train had left the station, the adventure had begun. You must convince the hero of your story to get on the train.

In storytelling terms one of the best examples is from one of my favourite films, *Back To The Future*. At the end of the movie, after an epic adventure, the hero, Marty, returns home and is about to enjoy a well-deserved break. He has barely slept, has almost been erased from history and is dazed and exhausted. Then his mentor, Doc Brown, shows up and says, 'Marty, you've got to come back with me... back to the future! Quick get in the car.' Marty jumps in the car. Imagine if the Doc had said, 'Quick Marty, we're going to work flat out for the next couple of weeks, travelling forwards and backwards in time, getting shot at and nearly killed, all in an attempt to solve a problem that won't happen for another thirty years!' I think Marty would have said, 'Actually I think I'll just relax with my girlfriend for a while and maybe call you when my head is unscrambled from our last death-defying adventure!'

When we're working with medical doctors and showing them how to turn case studies into compelling stories to improve patient treatments, the last step of the story is usually something like, 'The next time you see a male patient in his fifties with these symptoms, please consider using this treatment and let me know what results you get.' It is simple and achievable, not salesy.

Some people say that they're not in a position to tell others in the room what to do. Usually we discover that this is not actually the case. If you've been asked to present information to people more senior than you, then they want you to help them understand what the data means and what they should do about it. This includes the next steps. Without next steps, you're not communicating fully and your heroes won't actually know what to do with what you've told them. You may need to be respectful of seniority, but try finishing with a 'choose your own adventure'-type of story. You could say: 'Where do we go from here? There are a couple of options that would move us in the direction you're aiming for, which are A and B. I'll leave the decision up to you.' Note, though, that if you do use this kind of ending, don't make it sound like an ultimatum. It's not a case of take your advice or perish. Being given a choice leaves us feeling empowered; being threatened just makes us resist.

CREATE YOUR STORY

Who is your audience? (This is the hero; you are the mentor.)

What challenges is your audience concerned about?

....
....
....
....
....
....
....

What goals does your audience want to achieve?

....
....
....
....
....
....
....

What does your audience need from you? (Make sure you're thinking
win–win. People will sense if you're not and switch off.)

....
....
....
....
....
....
....

Now you're ready to create your story. In your own words describe your audience's current pain.

Describe a better future.

Explain how your audience can reach this better future, in 3 steps, including proof.

Step 1

Step 2

Step 3

Finish with 'The first step we can take to get things started is…'

When you have filled all of this in you have the basic structure for your story. However, don't create a word-for-word script. It won't feel natural if you read it. Even if you memorise it, you may sound stilted; and if your memory fails you, you'll panic. It's more helpful to write down trigger words – a few words under each section that will remind you of the key elements you want to cover.

The more you use storytelling, the easier it will become. Eventually, when somebody asks for your opinion in a meeting you'll be able to explain your thoughts in this way, without any notes or preparation, keeping them hooked from start to finish.

Storytelling in action

You can even use storytelling to change how your whole team communicates. I once trained a team of analysts that needed to turn its business insights into action. The team members decided to use this story structure for every email they sent to each other, plus for every team meeting. I then trained every agency who provided the analysts with data, so that they were all using story to communicate. They say it transformed their thinking and then their business.

When I meet new clients, I use the story structure to guide our conversation. I go in with a blank notebook and no agenda. I just guide the conversation with questions that build the story. I ask about what challenges they have, what they would like the future to look like, then I describe a journey we can take to achieve this and suggest a first step. After winning the work, they often tell us that they met other companies who pitched using slides, handouts and bullet points. They chose us because we listened and told compelling stories.

I'm not against using slides or handouts, but I urge you to use this story structure first. Don't make the mistake of creating a bunch of slides then hoping to work out a story later. When you're happy with the words of your story, you're ready to venture into the next chapter to enhance your message with visual storytelling.

Chapter 10
You were born visual

'Don't be ridiculous! Of course you need the screen!' My client thought I was deluded. I had just asked the hotel staff to take the projector and screen out of our meeting room, as we wouldn't be using them. 'How are you going to teach us to do presentations if you aren't using any slides?' she asked.

'Your slides are not your presentation,' I assured her. 'You are.'

For the first eight years that I coached clients, I didn't own a laptop, let alone use any slides. I used to walk into meeting rooms, turn off the projector and speak to people. This gained some great reactions, including one person who said, 'Thank goodness! Finally somebody is actually going to talk to us!'

The hotel client, though, explained that the screen was her crutch and she would be lost without it. When I told her that I would be teaching her team how to communicate successfully without it, she was intrigued. Everyone left the workshop elated. They realised that we can all connect and communicate without projectors. They were determined to reduce the use of slides in their business.

Use slides if you wish. Just don't rely on them. When a large screen is on offer some people find their natural instincts for communication fall apart and they are lured in by the temptation to make the screen do all the work, while they hide at the side of the room. Even though technology is designed to empower you (and it can), it more often leads to the suffocation and eventual death of ideas.

I'm sure you've heard the phrase 'death by PowerPoint'. Maybe you've experienced it for yourself, sitting in a meeting and watching a bunch of slides that made you lose the will to live. How did our slides become so bad that we're killing people with them? I mean, it's not called 'bruised by PowerPoint'. Nope. Death. I'm sure that the creators of this software had no intention of killing ideas in meetings across the world, so what went wrong?

In order to figure this out, we need to get back to basics for a minute. I'd like you to imagine that I was trying to describe something that you'd never heard of before. If I said I was about to show you 'visual aids' you should have two expectations: first, that I'm going to show you something visual; second, that it is going to help (aid) you. Using these rules we could delete almost every slide ever created around the world.

Let's be honest, what usually goes on a slide? That's right – your script. What else? A leave-behind-document. Anything else? Perhaps a little clip-art image in the corner, trying to save the slide. It won't save it. The idea has already died.

What if there were another way to use visual aids? What if you could achieve more, in less time, and escape the dreadful bullet points of the past? What if you could make all your content 550 percent more memorable with a simple method, backed by science?

You can – by becoming a visual storyteller.

BRAIN RULES FOR PRESENTATIONS

In his book *Brain Rules*, Dr John Medina explains the P.S.E. – Pictorial Supremacy Effect. A test carried out in Washington, D.C. proved that if you give a presentation while showing people text (such as words on a presentation slide), just three days later they will retain only 10 percent of the information. However, if you give the same presentation while showing them images, three days later they will remember 65 percent.

Just imagine applying this to your next pitch, speech or webinar. Instead of filling your slides with deadly bullets and words that drain attention and distract us from hearing your message, do this:

- Write your script.

- Think long and hard – do you **really** need to use a slide?

- If you do, then use an image. (Put your notes on a piece of paper in front of you. Put additional information in a document for people to read later.)

Slides are not essential. They are optional.

- You must have great content to say.

- You must deliver it well.

- You **might** need some slides or visual aids. Or you might not.

I eventually started using visual aids when I realised that there were some powerful images I could show people to help the learning stick. I also included music and video clips to further boost people's memory of the key messages.

Most people just fall into the lazy habit of thinking, 'I've got a presentation to do, I'll write my notes on slides so that I can remember what to say and then print that out to give people as a handout.'

Nobody wants your slide-u-ment! They don't want to read it on the screen. They don't want to read it afterwards. They certainly don't want to watch you read it to them. One man at a conference actually stood up part way through a talk, where the speaker was simply repeating what was written on the slides. The man shouted, 'We can all f%$@ing read! Are you going to say anything that isn't on your slide? If not, you can email me the slides and we can all go home.' The speaker confirmed that he would just be talking through what was written on the screen and the man left. The rest of the audience left with him mentally and emotionally, but owing to politeness they stuck it out physically, quietly looking in his direction, waiting for him to finish.

Many people have asked me over the years how to make their talks more lively so that their audiences stop falling asleep! They are hoping for a gimmick, a hack, a trick they can strap on to their talk that will rescue it. The truth requires more work. You need to speak the way you were born to speak, create stories in the way that people are born to listen and use images to help people understand and remember your message.

Almost half our brain is devoted to visual perception. One study showed that people who were asked to look at 2,500 images for just ten seconds per image, could remember 90 percent of them three days later. Amazingly, they could still recall 63 percent a year later. A year! Could the same be said for the last slide deck you sat through? If it was filled with bullets and words, there's not a chance.

'People can pay attention for only forty minutes at a time...'

Have you heard this nonsense before? I'm not sure where or when this started, but there's a myth that we have tiny attention spans. If I am speaking at an event, I will often do a two-hour session for a large audience. On the day of the event, the conference organiser will rush up to me and say, 'I hear you'll be speaking for two hours. When would you like the coffee break?'

I reply by saying, 'Either before or after my session.' They think I've lost my mind. 'What do you mean? You can't speak for two hours with no break! People can't pay attention for that long!'

Some of them get very insistent about this and so I feel the need to reassure them. 'Have you ever been to the movies?' Yes, they tell me. 'Movies hold our attention for two hours because they tell visual stories that engage our emotions. I'll be doing the same thing.' You can do this too.

SPLIT FOCUS

If you place words on a screen while you're talking to people you're creating an impossible task. People will assume that you want them to read the words, otherwise why would you put them there? At the same time you continue to talk and they want to listen to you. So should they read or listen? No matter which one they choose, they'll feel as if they have missed out, or they'll become mentally exhausted by attempting to do both.

The parts of your brain that deal with reading and listening are close together – they can't function fully at the same time. However, if you ask people to look at images while talking to them, they can do this perfectly well. The mind is much more adept at instantly taking in vast amounts of information from an image, while it's listening to what someone is saying.

Given this, it stunned me to find out that textbooks exist that teach the '1, 7, 7' approach to creating slides. They advise to put one title at the top of each slide, then seven bullets, with seven words per bullet. Fifty words a slide! If you have a hundred slides, people have to read a 5,000-word document while you talk. It's not going to happen!

Just consider how difficult it is to get your friend or partner's attention when they're busy reading something. If they continue to look at their book while you say something important, how does that make you feel? Ignored? Worthless? So why would anyone do this to themselves with presentation slides?

Have you guessed the answer? It took me a while to figure this one out. Time and again we find that people create lengthy text-filled slides because they're afraid of being the centre of attention and of forgetting what to say. They don't want people looking at them. So they give the audience something else to look at.

Most conference rooms have a massive screen on one wall. The person who is speaking is often hidden behind a wooden box at the side of the room. Just in case there was some danger that people might look at the speaker, they use a laser-pointer to show people exactly where they should be looking – at the hundreds of words, graphs and charts that are packed full of information that nobody could possibly remember. Death indeed!

There are a few other challenges, which I'll quickly summarise:

- It's a team presentation and everyone else in your team wants to share a slide-deck. How can you get them to stop using text on the slides? Put the words in the presenter notes below the slides, or in a document. Not on the screen.

- Perhaps your clients like words on a screen? No, they don't. We give coaching to 10,000 people every year and nobody ever says they like slides. That's your perception. What they want is good content, well delivered.

Words on slides kill your flow, kill the message, kill the attention of the audience, kill the memory of your message. In short, bullets kill. Don't put them on the screen. Print them, don't project them.

In future, if someone asks you to email them your presentation, the answer is no. You are the presentation. You are the reason for the meeting. People don't go to meetings to see slides. They will be there to see you communicate the message physically, vocally and through a storytelling structure that gives meaning to the information.

YOU LOOK, WE LOOK

So what should your relationship be with the screen? How do you use a screen effectively as a great storyteller?

Whether you have images on your slide or not, there is a simple rule in holding the audience's focus. Every time you look at the slide, we will also look at it. This is true in conversations too – if we are talking and you turn to look intently at something, we will turn to look at it as well.

You can use this to your advantage to direct the attention of people around you. When you want us to look at your image, simply step back and turn to look at it. When you turn back to us we will look at you. You can then talk, knowing that we have seen the image and we are now listening to you, wanting to know how this image fits into your story.

'My content is really serious. I can't just use images, can I?'

I'd like you to think about the most important information you receive on a daily basis. It is gathered by experts in communication, who want to make sure you understand the complex issues from around the world. They'll help you to remember it through storytelling and images. Who are these people? News presenters.

Switch on the news this evening and watch how brilliant journalists put together critical issues in a memorable format. The presenter takes up most of the screen. Behind them you may see an image that helps you to understand the story. The only time anyone puts text on the screen is when the content is designed to be aired in airports, hospital waiting rooms and office lobbies... with the sound off. For the main evening news, a presenter is front and centre with an image behind. At no point does the presenter say, 'I put my script up here on the screen beside me in bullet points so that we can read it together.' They have the script in front of them and images behind them.

If you want a printed handout of the news, you can buy a newspaper. It would seem ridiculous for a news presenter to just hold up a copy of the paper and say, 'I ran out of time to create this show, so I just put my notes, slides and printed document together. I'll just read from this and then give you a copy.'

DO IT LIKE THE PROFESSIONALS

Following the standard set by news presenters, you need three things:

- Your notes, in the form of a story.

- Images that help people remember your information.

- A document that you can email or give to people for further reading.

Then you're ready to deliver your story. You take the lead. The screen will support you, a bit like Batman and Robin. You are Batman and the visual aids are Robin, the handy sidekick who occasionally helps out. If you let your slides become Batman, then you may as well email them and save yourself the time and cost of the meeting.

Some of the best Batman stories don't even include Robin. You could forget visual aids altogether, or perhaps turn off the screen for part of your talk. On most laptops you can press the letter 'B' to blank the slide, so that you can have a conversation without distractions. You can also pop up a holding slide, or your logo, in between sections. This way, you're running the slides, the slides aren't running you.

WHEN TO USE A VISUAL AID

If you can describe your information clearly without an image, then do it. If you can't, then one of these may help:

- Props: whenever possible bring the physical thing you're talking about to your meeting. It is much more visceral than a slide.

- Graphs: these must visually represent your data in a way that is easy to understand. Before you create the graph consider what message your audience needs to receive from it. Check that people will gain the insight they need with just a quick glance.

- Images: use these to prove your message, or make it memorable.

- Flipcharts or displays: use these to highlight aspects of your ideas. But have them on display only when they're useful, so that they don't disrupt your connection with people.

GRAPHS DON'T NEED TO BE FANCY

Graphs can be very powerful, if used properly. They're terrific for displaying numerical data in a visual way.

But wait! I know what you're thinking. Your computer software has loads of funky options that can jazz up your graphs and make them look more exciting. That isn't the point. The goal is clarity.

I was once working with a telecommunications company and saying that boring graphs were often better than fancy ones. I explained that it's better to avoid three-dimensional graphs, because they often make it much harder to understand the information. One attendee agreed: 'Yes, exactly. That's what my manager is always telling me – if the numbers are bad, then make the graph 3D and nobody will know!' This is not what I'm suggesting!

If you use a graph, don't just copy and paste one from your data. Think very carefully about what message people need to take away from this data. Then work out the best way to represent it visually. It might be a graph that allows people to see one crucial number clearly.

Sometimes a graph is not the solution. Perhaps you've noticed that the numbers of people buying one of your products has gradually risen from 80 to 20,000. You could put that on a graph if you want, or you could show an image of a bus and a football stadium. This will grab people's attention far more, especially when you say, 'In 2010, the number of people who were buying this product filled just one bus. Today, our customers would fill a stadium.' Pictures grab the audience and convey the message far better than a graph.

DOES IT NEED TO BE BEAUTIFUL?

The focus here isn't on beautifully lit photographs. It's on visual storytelling. You can do that without photos. Some of the most memorable slides I've seen were created in the space of thirty seconds. One attendee at one of my workshops had delivered a short talk in the morning to a group of his colleagues. At the end of his presentation, I asked him to explain his role within the company. There were chuckles around the room. Somebody said, 'Good question. We can't figure out what he does either!'

He tried to explain his role and I honestly still didn't understand. Later that day we talked about using compelling visual aids to explain a message. The man came up to me and said, 'Could I just get a few minutes to re-design my slides from earlier?'

I assured him that this wasn't necessary, as we were still focussed on coaching people on their delivery style. 'Thirty seconds, then?!' he insisted. He rushed off, tapped on his keyboard and came back to the front of the room. And then he wowed us all. 'I know you are all confused about what I do. So let me explain. What I do is take this...'

RISK

'And I turn it into this.'

RISK

'Ah! I get it now! That's what you do!' No photos, just imagination and font size. At no point did he say, 'I reduce risk and while we can't remove risk completely we can make problems much smaller and more manageable.' He didn't have to. His visual aid did it for him.

DON'T RELY ON 'STOCK PHOTOS'

By this point you may be feeling the urge to rip up a recent pitch, speech or presentation and start a new slide deck with images flying in all directions. For every image, remember to check:

- Do you really need it?
- Will it make your key ideas more memorable?
- Does that image really make sense and help your message, or are you just using it for the sake of having an image?

Some images that I've seen make absolutely no sense. You could stare at them for ever and not know what they mean. These images tend to lead to three possible outcomes during a talk:

Rarely: the image is used to build curiosity. The presenter allows the audience to look at the screen for a moment before telling them what the image means. The whole room says 'Aah!! I get it!' In which case you've chosen a great image that your audience will remember.

Or

Mostly: the speaker doesn't mention what the image is because they think it's obvious, it's pretty or they don't know why it's there. (I recently saw a talk where an audience member raised a hand and asked, 'What's that on your slide?' The speaker had no idea; someone else had created the slides. And at that point the whole room stopped listening. We had lost confidence in his knowledge.)

Or

Sometimes: the speaker explains what the image is for and people in the room collectively think 'Huh? Really? I don't get it.'

If you end up with option 2 or 3, you're damaging your message. Make the clearest choice you can. If in doubt, test your image on a few people before you speak to a more important crowd, to see if it makes sense. Does it help? Is it memorable? If so, use it. If not, bin it.

HOW MANY SLIDES?

Following many years of death by PowerPoint, lots of meetings are now preceded by a memo that says, 'No more than ten slides please.' What impact does that have? People take their fifty slides and cram all of that information onto ten slides, making the font size so small that you would need a magnifying glass to make sense of it. The memo just makes death by PowerPoint more painful.

Thinking about the number of slides you use is to miss the point. The number of slides, the frequency and the ideal amount are all dependent on what your message needs; what your audience needs.

I've seen brilliant talks given with no slides and others with six slides per minute. Conversely, I've seen confusing talks that desperately needed an image to make sense of a concept. No matter how many slides you have, one thing is always true: have only one key idea per slide. Don't stuff loads of things together and make people play *Where's Wally?* (Or *Where's Waldo* if you're in North America.)

If you're using a laser that's your first clue that there's too much on your slide. A laser is used when a speaker is saying, 'I know there's loads of stuff up on the screen, but the bit I really want you to notice is this bit.' Forget it. Create a new slide with just the information that your audience needs at that moment in your presentation. No laser, just a laser-like focus. Say only what people need to hear; use only images that will help them remember the message.

Persuading others to go slide-free

Demand that everyone at your company buys and reads this book immediately and then applies everything they learn. (Just kidding – you should buy the book for them.)

Seriously, though, if you're working on a project with a group of people who seem intent on using as many slides as possible, there are three things you can try:

- Take all the words off the slides and put them into the 'presenter notes' section;

- Or, have just one key idea per slide;

- Or, if all else fails, create 'builds', so that you gradually add elements to your slide, instead of showing everything at once.

Otherwise, you need to persuade them that your presentation will be stronger if you can:

- Turn off the screen – you don't need a screen to communicate with people. Do as many meetings as you can without any visual aids. Turn off the screen when you don't need it, even midway through a talk. Use it only if it genuinely helps the person you're meeting to understand and remember your ideas.

- Use images, graphics and props. No text. The process for deciding whether or not you need these visual aids should be:

a) Write a script.

b) If you need them put images on a screen, or bring props.

c) Create a separate printed document, if you need one. This can include the images, plus a summary of your main points.

Tell your collaborators about the news presenters: a script in front of them, images behind them, a newspaper as a printed document.

If your co-workers think all this sounds like a lot of effort, when they would rather just stick loads of bullet points up on a screen and read them, try the following.

HOW MUCH EFFORT?

To help you appreciate how much effort you should put into creating a compelling story and powerful visuals, consider this – how many people are you speaking to and how long are you speaking for? If you're talking to twenty people for an hour, then you are actually going to communicate for twenty individual hours. That's a lot of people hours, and a lot of investment in what you have to say. It's important that you prepare to deliver something worthwhile.

That sounds like a lot of pressure, right? And that's why it's important to hold your nerve and stay calm and focussed when you communicate an important message, even when you're feeling stressed inside. It's time to talk about State.

PART 3
STATE

Chapter 11
You were born to thrive

My body couldn't move. My mind was a blur. I had lost the capacity to make sounds. The people around me seemed like distant objects. I was on stage, doing a performance of the play *The Ghost Train*, suffering paralysing stage fright.

I was playing the Station Master of the old, haunted railway station and was about to give my long speech to a group of stranded travellers about the deadly fate that would come to any person who stayed there overnight. This speech sets up the play, letting the audience know what the story is all about. It is essential to the plot and without it the events that follow don't make any sense.

Just before the first performance, my character's moustache went missing. It was a magnificent walrus moustache that almost took over my face. It was perfect for the person I was playing and helped me get into character. I was given a tiny, thin replacement to use instead. The last-minute change made me feel distracted and annoyed as I went on stage to start the play on opening night.

As the moment for my speech arrived, my replacement moustache began to peel off my face. Under the heat of the stage lights, the glue melted. Unsure what to do, I lost focus and forgot the first line of my speech. I froze. Silence fell. The rest of the cast stared at me aghast. The same fear of speaking that I had felt at school a few years before swelled up within me. My blood drained from my face. My legs wouldn't move. I couldn't see straight.

Eventually, another actor repeated his line, asking why they shouldn't stay at the station, hoping to prompt me back into action. My mind screamed at me 'Don't mess this up again! Everyone is watching, they will think you're a failure. They probably already do. You're not as good as everyone else. It's over. Quit now! Run!!'

Yet another actor repeated the question, in a slightly different way, trying to hint at what I should say. It brought me back to the present moment. I somehow murmured a rough version of the events that I was supposed to describe, all the while looking and feeling as if at any moment I may fall off the stage. I got to the end and finally it was time for someone else to speak. I left the stage. I stood behind the set, angry that I had messed up after working so hard to memorise my lines. Then silence fell again. While I was beating myself up about making a mistake, I had missed my next line as well!

I was supposed to pop my head out of the Station Master's hatch and add another important message, but I didn't. The cast realised I was absent and kept going. I was devastated. I had let everyone down. Twice. And I had failed myself. I finally managed to get back on stage, but every word sounded tense, as if I was forcing the words out, panicked that I would lose the ability to speak at any moment.

After the play finished and the audience had left, we were all brought back on stage. The director wanted to talk to me with the rest of the cast about what happened. Everything he said made sense. 'If you forget your lines just describe the story as best you can. If you make a mistake don't worry about it, just move on. If you see another actor losing their lines (or their mind) just fill in for them and keep going. The show must go on.'

But none of it helped. I knew all of these things. My regular, logical mind wasn't functioning. My monkey mind had taken over.

THE MONKEY MIND

There are moments in all our lives that we really want to go well – an important pitch, interview, date or speech. These are the days when we most need to thrive, yet, sadly, from my experience, these are the situations when we are most likely to lose control. Why? I wanted to understand this from an evolutionary perspective, so I read *The Chimp Paradox* by Dr Steve Peters.

Peters explains that the emotional mind (remember: our brain is made up of a logical part and an emotional part) is not designed to make us happy and help us succeed. It is designed to keep us alive. When we are stressed, the body reads that we are in danger and our emotions take over. As a result we prepare to fight or flee. Everything other than the urge to fight or flee – such as the need to remember lines in a play – shuts down.

Dr Peters used the essence of *The Chimp Paradox* to coach the British Olympic cycling team to victory in 2012. He once mentioned that cyclist Victoria Pendleton asked him, 'How do you kill the monkey in your head?' He replied by saying that you can't kill it, but you can learn to tame it, befriend it and keep it under control.

Another great author on the subject is Timothy Gallwey, who wrote the *Inner Game* book series. He explains that in all situations our performance should be exactly the same as our potential... but it isn't. Mental interference gets in the way, derailing us. He put this into a simple calculation:

Performance = potential minus interference

The 'interference' may include a voice in your head – the monkey mind. It may jabber away, saying negative things to persuade you to flee the situation, to keep you safe from harm, such as, 'Don't trust them, why did you wear that shirt today, you're failing, leave now before you humiliate yourself... .' In the case of my railway play, my monkey mind reacted badly to the moustache debacle, and triggered my underlying fear of performing badly in front of my fellow actors, my audience and any agents. The moustache was my armour. Losing it left me feeling vulnerable. I allowed it to destabilise me very badly.

At times of intense stress, the body releases the stress hormone cortisol, which interferes with the functioning of the hippocampus in the brain. This is where we store our memories. When cortisol takes over, we lose access to basic information. This frequently happens in exams, interviews and on stage. My monkey mind took hold, cortisol went up and – boom! – my lines were gone.

I was determined never to let people down in this way again. I wanted to discover how to get past the monkey mind, settle him down and allow my natural ability to come through when I needed it. What follows are the techniques I have developed to give people the best results under pressure. No matter how much anxiety you feel about public speaking, or speaking up in a meeting or at an important event, you can apply the steps that follow to ensure you perform at your best when you need to.

STEP ONE – PEAK STATE VS. POOR STATE

In 2011 Rory McIlroy was an intimidating presence in golf and a celebrated champion. He was playing in the Augusta Championship and had a four-shot lead as he went into the final day. All he had to do was keep playing the sport he loved and he would win.

He finished in tenth place. Later he explained he had lost his confidence, so his match unravelled on the last few holes. Eight weeks later he won the US Open. What happened in between? Did he learn how to hit a golf ball? No, he didn't need to. He simply went from a poor state to a peak state mindset.

Tennis ace Serena Williams went through a similar thing. She had been a dominant force on the courts, ranked first among female tennis players. Then an injury caused her ranking to drop to number 172. After the injury, she still had extraordinary skills, but described being fearful of defeat. She had some mindset coaching to get back into a peak state. In 2015 she won fifty-three out of fifty-six matches; in 2016 she became the most successful female tennis player in history.

When have you been in a poor state or peak state?

It's completely normal for us to feel anxious before an important meeting or event. The trouble is that our anxiety alerts the monkey mind, which may search our internal database for similar situations when we've felt anxious and then replay them over and over. The monkey wants us to avoid failure or rejection and is attempting to save us from further pain. In sports this may cause an athlete to 'choke'. In speech delivery, it's our voice that gets choked.

Think back through your life for a moment. When have you had a peak-state experience? What about a poor state? These don't need to be situations when you won something or when you failed at something. It's more about how you felt. Did you perform at your best or were you shackled by fear? Keep thinking about when you have had situations like this, while I give you some examples.

After leaving acting school I had peak-state and poor state experiences within the space of one week. I was given the opportunity to try out for the lead role in a feature film. As I went to the first-round audition, I was so convinced that I wouldn't get the role that I felt no worries at all. I was free to just be myself, relax and enjoy the experience. My acting skills were well-honed after years of studying and performing, so I just went into the audition room, gave my chosen performance and breezed out again feeling great about how it went. My mind was in a peak state, with no expectation about what may happen and no attachment to the outcome.

To my surprise the director rushed back out and said, 'We want to see you again next week.' I was shocked. Other, more experienced actors were in the waiting room and looked up from their scripts in a similar state of surprise. My stomach dropped. My brain froze. I had shifted from peak state to poor state in just a few seconds.

The following week all I could think was, 'Me? The lead in a feature-length movie? But I only just graduated from college?! I can't do this!' When I went back to the second audition I was paired up with a stunning actress who had moved over from Hollywood to take her shot in the London acting scene. She seemed completely unimpressed when she was asked to perform a scene with me. 'Even she knows I'm not ready for this role,' I thought.

We were called in and did the scene. The director looked bemused. 'Could... could you do it like you did it last week? You know, relaxed, charming...' Nope. My monkey mind had other ideas. I blew it. I tensed up. I showed them what I believed – that I didn't belong there. The director asked me to leave.

This switch from peak state to poor state happened because I had limited my belief. I thought I wasn't ready for that kind of success. The director thought I was. My monkey mind freaked out.

There are other, faster triggers that can kick you into a poor state almost immediately, when your monkey is trying to avoid past pain, sabotaging your behaviour in the process. As you read through the following story, start thinking about what triggers you have. What sort of things can tip you into a poor state?

One of my triggers used to be a major fear of blushing. It was such a big issue for me that I avoided brightly lit places, so that it would be less obvious if it happened. I always wanted to have an exit from a room or conversation, so that if I felt like I might blush, I would be able to make my excuses and leave.

I knew that I was more likely to blush if I was criticised, so I worked incredibly hard to make sure that every event I ran was perfect. That way people would have nothing to criticise. Then I found myself at an event that sent the monkey on the rampage in my brain!

Monkey triggers

I was booked to do an event in Washington, D.C. The lady who hired me had seen me before at an event in Paris that had gone tremendously well. She got in touch a few months later, wanting me to teach her team. There would be fifty people attending and I would have four hours with them. She knew what I needed and so I had no concerns about the event. I was really looking forward to it. No monkey mind issues. Or so I thought. While I didn't have any limiting beliefs about how well the event would go, I did still have some negative triggers that could tip me from peak state to poor state very quickly.

I always like to have a big room, a large screen and plenty of space for activities, as my sessions tend to be quite lively and interactive. I arrived about ninety minutes before my event would start, so that I had plenty of time to get ready. They took me to a corridor and said, 'We thought we would do the session here.' Huh?!

They didn't have a room big enough for our event, so people were just going to bring their chairs into the corridor to listen to me. Okay, I thought, no big deal. I can make this work. I'm more than happy to work around challenges. I had done an event in a corridor before at a conference in Oxford. They had run out of breakout spaces, so I just stood there with 300 people sat in front of me for an hour. It all went well. The major difference was that the conference centre had far more space. The office in D.C. was tiny, with a low ceiling, narrow corridors and large pillars blocking the view.

Next up – the screen. They had a small TV, on a tiny stand, which meant that people beyond the first two rows wouldn't be able to see it. Plus it didn't like my computer. The slides wouldn't come up. After scrabbling around on the floor with cables, I finally left their tech guy to fix it while I went to the bathroom, knowing that I had about forty minutes left until my session. It was plenty of time to get everything else ready to create a terrific event.

Five minutes later I came back and found a sea of chairs in front of me with fifty expectant people sitting in them. They filled every bit of the corridor, leaving only tiny amounts of room for me to stand in. If you've seen me speak, you'll know that I move around a lot to run activities with people. The lack of room was a challenge.

The ceiling lights were on full brightness and it was a low ceiling. There was no way for me to get to the screen without climbing over people and certainly no way to exit if I wanted to. There was even a camera filming the session and streaming it live across the country, so I worried that if I messed up, people I would never meet would be laughing at me.

The organiser started to introduce me, saying they had decided to start the session early. News to me. My equipment wasn't ready. My heart was pounding, my head felt warm, but it would be okay. I would just start, get in the zone and everything would be fine.

She introduced me by saying, 'I've seen this guy before and he is outstanding. He is easily the best speaker I have ever seen and so I know that this session will be the best coaching you will ever receive. We've paid a high price to fly him all the way over from England and so he'd better be good! Here he is... ' As generous as it is to get a big introduction like that, I have always preferred something low key. I often joke that the favourite introduction that I've ever had at a conference was when a lady stood up and said, 'Last year we had a really expensive, famous, Olympic Gold medallist, who was amazing. This year we couldn't afford it, so we've just got Richard. Here he is...' I loved this. It made me laugh, but I also knew how powerful it was. My aim is always to exceed people's expectations. If they start by thinking you'll be terrible, then it's really easy to wow them.

In Washington, D.C. they were expecting a dazzling show that would leave them in a profound state of euphoria. Anything less would be disappointing.

I began the session and all was going fine for about thirty seconds. Then my laptop stopped working. This had never happened before, nor has it happened since. It froze and there was nothing I could do to fix it. Fifty sets of eyes stared at me in silence, along with hundreds of people watching live online, as I tried to fix it, under the bright lights with rows of people bunched up against me.

Nothing seemed to work. As time went by, in the silence of the staring eyes, my monkey had a meltdown. Sweat started pouring down my face and my back. My face went bright red. My hands were shaking. I finally got the computer to restart and was ready to go. I took some deep breaths and stood up, determined to do my best and keep going. Then the organiser said, 'Oh dear, Richard. You look so sweaty! Do you need to take a shower before we start again?!' Raging monkey explosions happened in my head. I felt angry with myself, upset, confused and disappointed all at once.

Later on, I reflected on what happened in order to break down all of the triggers. I knew that I would be presenting to people again, so I would have to get past the monkey melt-down and ensure that next time I would be okay. The triggers were:

- Feeling unprepared, with the session starting early.

- Feeling hot and sweaty.

- Being surrounded, with no exit.

- Having a lack of space for my lively activities.

- Technology failing me.

The techniques in this chapter mean that these no longer overwhelm me. The triggers still come up sometimes (I'm not sure that they ever disappear completely), but now I have a whole range of strategies to get back into a peak state whenever I need to.

I had to put every strategy into action when I was later booked to speak at an event in Helsinki, Finland. I was told that I would have 200 people, a stage, a great technical crew to support me and an audience who had specifically chosen to see my session.

I always arrive extra early, just in case I need to fix or adjust something, but at this event the organiser insisted on driving me to the venue. He was late. Very late. Instead of getting there ninety minutes before my session, we had twelve minutes to spare. Monkey Trigger 1. I had to run the last part of the journey with a heavy suitcase and was left feeling hot, sweaty and out of breath. Monkey Trigger 2.

Then, they showed me the stage. I was expecting the typical conference room with a proper stage. They had a small square podium... in the middle of a corridor. Monkey Trigger 3.

There were no seats by the stage, so I asked if they were sure if I was in the right place. Yes, they said, it was a 'freestyle' event and so people would just stop walking past and stand for a few minutes. My sessions are interactive, with lengthy activities that require sitting and standing as people practise techniques. The material I had prepared wasn't going to work. Monkey Trigger 4.

I explained that I needed to plug in my laptop and play videos and music, all of which we had agreed a few days before. They looked surprised and said it was impossible. We spent eleven minutes trying to get the technology to work and finally found a solution, but with one major problem. There were four screens attached to a stand above my head, pointing away from me and so I had no idea what was being shown on them at any given time. There was no way for me to tell if what I was saying matched the images that people could see. The technology had failed me again. Monkey Trigger 5.

I had sixty seconds left to get into a peak state in order to avoid defeat, humiliation and pain. I employed every technique that I'm about to share with you and felt ready to do my best work.

If I'd had any more time to re-think I may have backed out or changed my content, but I had no time. I just had to believe with total confidence that some Finnish people walking by might stop for long enough to hear the instructions to one of the activities, otherwise I would end up looking like a crazed mad man!

But people did stop. And stayed. And looked amused by this funny English guy who seemed totally convinced that everyone in the exhibition centre was listening and would take part in some wild activities in front of a bunch of strangers. And they did. What had appeared at first to be my worst nightmare turned into an unexpected success and one of my proudest moments, with Tweets and emails afterwards saying, 'You Rock!', as well as many people stopping to shake my hand and say how much they enjoyed it. One lady even said that my talk had inspired and empowered her to change careers.

This event (and many others like it) showed me that you can get into a peak state despite what is happening around you. I believe that Americans call this 'embracing the suck'. When you have tough events in your life, you can either get miserable and depressed or embrace them and decide to learn all that you can from them. You can turn them into your biggest successes. I encourage you to feel empowered by challenges, always be learning from them and that way you'll be stronger each day.

Now let's go through the specific techniques that can help you when you face challenges like these, so that you can overcome your own monkey mind and become the best version of yourself when you need to.

Peak-state memories

Think back to a situation where you have been in a peak state. By this I mean a situation where you felt confident, in control and able to perform at your best. You can choose any situation you like, from school, work or your personal life. It doesn't matter if you succeeded in that situation (such as a job interview or sports game), it only matters that you felt like you were 'in the zone' or however you would describe the feeling of being in a peak state – the best version of you.

Start making a list of moments when you felt this way. This may trigger memories from many years ago, when you went on a date, had an interview, did a sales pitch, or played a sport, when you felt absolutely on your game. I personally keep a mental list of all the great moments like these, so that I can replay them in my mind before important events.

What's the benefit of this? Well, you'll remember that earlier on I was talking about the monkey getting scared when it notices you're anxious and so it focusses on all the memories of situations when you felt stressed and replays them over and over to help you avoid more pain. You need to give the monkey something better to watch.

When you have an important event coming up and you start to feel anxious, think back to moments when you felt in a peak state. This sounds way too easy to actually work, but I assure you it does. Give your monkey mind something reassuring, empowering and inspiring to replay. Add one event on top of another event. Add more events whenever you have a great peak-state experience, so that the monkey will have more to watch.

Ideally, in my experience, it works best if you replay an event that is similar to the one you are about to be in. If I am about to speak to a group of 100 people sitting at round tables, I search my memories for the same kind of situation that went well. However, when you're first building up the experience of speaking in front of people, you won't have these. That's okay, you don't need them. What you need to focus on is moments when you felt at your best, in order to trigger a peak-state performance. Let's check out the science on this...

The milkshake experiment

Alia Crum is a psychologist and researcher at the University of Columbia. She has been studying the placebo effect for many years. It is widely known in the medical field that people respond to medication partly through believing that it will help them.

(The power of the placebo was explored in great detail in the book *Cure* by award-winning science writer Jo Marchant. For example, people respond far better to a blue and red capsule given to them by a doctor in a white coat, than they do to a simple white pill they take themselves, even if neither pill has any physical medical benefit.)

Alia decided to find out if the placebo effect would apply to food labels. Ghrelin, the hunger hormone, controls our appetite. The more of it there is circulating in our body, the more hungry we feel. Once we eat, levels fall and we don't feel hungry any more.

Have you ever gone on a diet where you felt hungry all the time? Perhaps you kept saying to yourself, 'These vegetables and salad will never fill me up!' and sure enough after your meal you still felt hungry. It turns out that our beliefs about what we're eating control the levels of ghrelin in our body.

In the milkshake experiment, Alia gave a group of people a 'Sensishake' – zero fat, zero sugar and only 140 calories. Their ghrelin was tested before and after they drank it. This showed that their hunger levels barely changed.

The following week the same people were asked to drink another milkshake called 'Decadence You Deserve' – 56g of sugar, 30g of fat and 620 calories! Their ghrelin levels dropped significantly, taking their hunger feelings away. The surprise? It was the same drink, with a different label. So remember: if you go on a diet, make sure you change your beliefs about what foods satisfy you, otherwise those hunger feelings will remain even when your body is full.

We can control how we feel by changing what we focus on and believe when we're speaking too, by switching focus from poor-state experiences to peak-state experiences.

The stress test

There are two hormones that can cause you to lose your cool when you want to perform at your best. We've mentioned them both before: they are cortisol and adrenaline, the stress hormones. They cause your monkey mind to freak out.

Psychologists David Cresswell and David Sherman ran a series of experiments to see if they could help people get the monkey mind under control in situations of high stress. In the first study, known as the Trier Social Stress Test (TSST), they asked two groups of people to give a speech in front of a panel of judges, who had been instructed to give no positive reactions. The first group was told to write a full page about a deep personal value, such as being a good father, honesty, trying your hardest, or any other value that meant something important to them. The other group was told to write about something that they didn't care about. Both groups were then asked to give a speech about what they'd written. Once that was over, both groups were given a tough maths challenge while the panel continually said, 'Go faster!'

The group who had written about something that meant nothing to them had a spike in their stress levels. However, the group who wrote about a meaningful value showed no change. Their cortisol levels were the same before and after the event. This showed that by focusing on your core values, you can stay in a peak state when you need to, centred in the best version of yourself.

In another study the researchers tested the adrenaline levels of students who were soon taking important exams. Half of them were asked to do positive affirmations, the others did not. Those who did nothing saw a significant increase in their adrenaline leading up to and during the exam. Those who had been doing positive affirmations stayed calm with no difference in adrenaline levels.

These experiments suggest that we can tame the monkey mind by focussing on the positive. I put this to the test. I wrote a paragraph about each of my three core values. Then I came up with a one-word trigger that would remind me what each of them is. I focus on these trigger words as I lead up to critical events when I need to stay in a peak state, despite the potential for feeling stressed. It has been amazing to me how simple and effective this is.

Let's try this out.

First, what is a value? Values are the behaviours, principles and attitudes that are the most meaningful to you. They help define who you are and how you make choices each day. They may relate to the things you are most passionate about. Incidentally, I have met lots of people who say that their core value is money. One such person was a young, aspirational business owner.

I told him there is no way that can be true. It never is. I asked why he wanted money. He said, 'Money might not seem that important to other people, but I grew up poor and now I have a wife and two children. I have to make sure I can pay our bills and put food on the table, so that I can look after them.' His core value wasn't money. It was looking after his family – that's what he wanted the money for. Another delegate at the same conference had no family – he insisted that money was definitely his core value. We dug a bit. It wasn't. He wanted money in order that he could order what he wanted in a restaurant, go on holiday wherever he wanted, choose whatever he pleased. His core value was freedom.

Other examples of core values are health and vitality, friendship, serving others, inspiring people, doing good work, being creative... the list goes on. I hope that your values are starting to bubble up in your mind. Here are mine:

- Polar bears: I have always cared about being a good father.
  I decided to never go on a second date with someone who I
  could not imagine loving, marrying and raising children with.
  I had to be very patient! But I was okay with that. It was a
  core value for me. I knew I was looking for my ideal partner,
  because to me being a good father means being a great
  husband. It also drove me to find a profession where I could do
  something I truly believed in, so that I would be able to show
  my children that they too could become all that they want to
  be. What do polar bears have to do with all that? When my
  boys were only five and two, they often wanted to play polar
  bears, which meant crawling on the floor, with one child riding
  on my back and the other snuggled safely beneath me. The
  game connected me to them and made us all laugh. That's why
  polar bears are my first core value.

- Afrikids: I mentioned this charity at the start of the book. I
  have been donating to them for many years now, as well as
  training their team. I care very much about supporting their
  projects to bring opportunity, health, safety and education to
  people who would not otherwise have it. Serving others has
  always been part of me and driven my choice of career – I
  always wanted to become a teacher or actor, so that I could
  educate, inspire and entertain people. I feel so glad to be able
  to do this and use my profession to support charitable causes.

Remembering this part of myself helps me stay focussed on the best version of me.

- Specsavers: standing on a round stage with 1,000 Specsavers employees surrounding me, all of whom seemed engaged and uplifted was very meaningful to me. This word centres me on my value to help teach and entertain people.

Those are my three values. Now, what are yours?

Peak-state memories

First, in order to shift your mindset away from a poor state, think back to peak-state experiences. Use this space to make a list of all your favourite peak-state experiences. Have fun with it – think back as far as you wish; try to think of experiences that you'll be able to relate to events when you'll need your peak-state mindset in the future. Once you've done this, move on to the Mindset Worksheet over the page to identify your core values and why they mean so much to you.

MINDSET WORKSHEET

Value 1 (e.g. being a good father)

....

....

Trigger word for Value 1.

....

Why is this value important to you? How has it shaped your life?

....

....

....

....

....

....

....

....

....

Value 2

....

....

Trigger word for Value 2.

....

Why is this value important to you? How has it shaped your life?

....

....

_____

_____

_____

_____

_____

_____

_____

_____

_____

_____

_____

Value 3

_____

_____

Trigger word for Value 3.

Why is this value important to you? How has it shaped your life?

_____

_____

_____

_____

_____

_____

_____

_____

_____

_____

_____

STEP TWO – TAKE CARE OF YOUR MONKEY MIND

You can tackle Step One in advance of an event. Step Two is about how to take care of your monkey mind before or during an event.

As you read, remember that everyone is different: we all have unique triggers that may panic our monkey. Some people love crowds, others hate them; some feel soothed by classical music, others can't stand it. As you read this section, have a think about which strategies may work best for you, based on your own monkey mind.

Introvert vs extrovert

I so often hear the misconception that introverts don't like people and extroverts are loud and annoying. Neither of these summaries is true. If you're unsure if you're introvert or extrovert, answer the following:

- What kind of situation helps you to recharge?
    - Extroverts tend to get their energy from being around others.
    - Introverts can feel drained from a day surrounded by people and need some time by themselves.
- How do you process ideas?
    - Do you like to chat with people about your ideas in order to clarify what you think? If so, you're more likely to be extrovert.
    - Do you think things through in your head? If so you're more likely to be an introvert. Introverts prefer to know the agenda before a meeting and plan their thoughts before they arrive.

Of course, you may be an extrovert in some ways or situations and an introvert in others, or anything in between. No one fits neatly into one box. Despite the stereotypes, I know lots of fun and gregarious people who are actually introverts. Equally, I know plenty of extroverts who have low self-confidence.

There is some debate about whether we're born this way or whether our approach to life comes from our life experience. It doesn't really matter – however you came to be who you are, it makes sense to tap into how you're most likely to respond to situations. Your monkey mind will feel more settled if you give it what it needs.

Usain Bolt is a clear extrovert. When he is about to race, he will often find a marshall or some fans to chat to, cracking jokes until moments before he gets into position. On the other hand, legendary swimmer Michael Phelps is more introvert. He arrives poolside for his races in headphones, looking at the floor, blocking out everyone around him. Only just before he gets up on the block to prepare for his dive do the headphones come off.

If you're an extrovert, you may feel better if you can find some people to chat to when you arrive at your meeting before the meeting itself begins. The energy of other people will help to bring you up and out of yourself (especially if you've had a long, solitary journey to get there) so that you hit the meeting feeling at your best. If there's no one around, try calling friends or colleagues to give you a boost before you start. Even small moments of engagement can lift you.

If you're an introvert, you could feel drained by being around a lot of people at an important event. I know I certainly do. I don't need company or small talk. I just want to check that the technology works and quietly gather my thoughts. But I also don't want to appear rude! So I arrive early and greet my hosts, then explain that I need some time to check the laptop and microphone. If I'm working at an event that requires several of my team, I'll often pair up with an extrovert. If people want to chat to us, the extrovert can engage with them, while I have a quiet moment to get ready. That way, we both get what we need.

Have a think about what you need in order to feel energised. If you're unsure, try different approaches. You'll then have proof of what helps you to feel settled and ready for action.

Self-talk

You can also calm your monkey mind through your choice of self-talk. If you're thinking 'I don't to do self-talk,' then you're doing it right now! We all have a little voice in our heads, our inner thoughts, the things we think but don't say. The monkey mind can get very chatty and loud when we're feeling stressed. It may say things like, 'This is going badly, that person isn't listening, I shouldn't have worn this outfit, what if I forget everything I want to say?' How you answer the monkey is key to turning things around. How often have you been in a stressful situation and someone has told you to calm down? I suspect you'll agree that it doesn't help! Why? It's because we have to be careful what we say to the monkey. If we're told to calm down, we start telling the monkey, 'I'm calm, I'm calm.' But, the monkey isn't fooled by this. He checks. He realises that everything in your body – your heart rate, your tense muscles, your fast, shallow breathing – is giving exactly the opposite message. He shouts louder that you're definitely not calm!

Just changing the words that you use can help. When athletes are interviewed after an important race or event, the interviewer often says something along the lines of, 'This was a really big event for you. Were you nervous before it started?' Successful athletes often respond by saying, 'No, I wasn't nervous. I was excited.' If you say this to yourself, your monkey mind will check if this is true. 'Fast heart rate, high breathing, tense stomach, yes those are all things you feel when you are excited!' It will feel convinced that you're about to do something good rather than scary, and leave you free to access your peak mindset. Other reassuring phrases to offer the monkey are:

'I'm in the right place.'

'I know what I'm doing.'

'I'm the right person for the job.'

'I've done this before, I can do it again.'

They must be statements that the monkey cannot disagree with. How could he argue if you tell him that you're in the right place? Or that you've done it before so you can do it again? You get the picture.

Water

Just like breathing, water is essential for our survival. Keeping some nearby helps settle your mind and avoids a dry mouth or croaky voice. If you need some don't apologise for it, ask for it and take your time, even if you're mid-flow.

You may have seen the video of US politician Marco Rubio, who has been haunted by a moment where he needed water while doing a live television broadcast. After the US President gives the State of the

Nation speech, the opposing party selects one person to do a speech on live TV explaining why they disagree with various points.

When Rubio was chosen to do this, he gave a fairly average response... up until the moment where he needed a drink. At that point he snatched a bottle that was nearby took a hurried, awkward swig and carried on as if nothing had happened. It was the main thing that people remembered and talked about when he finished. Not because he needed some water, but because he looked flustered and unsettled when he drank it. Imagine if he'd done the opposite. What if he'd calmly, slowly reached for the bottle and slowly taken a thoughtful sip, before continuing? He would have seemed in control, calm and more authoritative, even.

If you need water, take your time. The audience will wait. Don't apologise for it. I keep some close by, in a bottle with a lid, not a glass – just in case someone knocks it over (I learned the hard way). The water should be room temperature, because cold or hot water is not as good for quenching a dry mouth and lubricating your voice. Sip small amounts, little and often, before you start and during your talk.

Breathing

Your breath is a barometer of your state – when it is shallow and fast, you're nervous or afraid; when it is deep, regular and wholesome, you're calm. Thankfully, just as our state can influence our breathing, conscious breathing can influence our state.

Look back at the 5552 breathing exercise on page 93. Do this just before you begin your meeting and you will take control of your nerves. You can even use it when you're swimming with sharks.

I went on a snorkelling trip off the coast of Central America, near the barrier reef. It is the second largest barrier reef in the world, after the Great Barrier Reef in Australia. There were countless beautiful fish – including stingrays... and sharks.

I had never used a snorkel before. The guide showed me how, then said, as if it were the most natural piece of advice in the world, 'If the sharks come near you, don't worry, they are quite friendly. Just don't put your hands out as they may eat your fingers.'

Whaat???!!

'Oh, and stay relaxed, because they will sense if you feel afraid.' Those were his last words before jumping in.

My heart was pounding through my eyeballs. The rest of my group looked cool and relaxed, ready for a leisurely swim. All of them started getting in the water. I had to get myself together. I wasn't going to be the only person left in the boat. I knew what I had to do.

'Give me a minute,' I said, as calmly as I could muster. I looked at the horizon and the lapping waves. I breathed in a 5552 rhythm and waited for my stress to ease down. Then I thought, 'Maybe we won't see any sharks anyway, they'll probably swim away when they hear us splashing around.'

I jumped in, adjusted my mask and looked ahead of me under water. Two sharks were swimming swiftly, straight for me. The theme tune from *Jaws* started playing loudly in my head.

I remembered the guide's advice – don't show them fear or fingers. I put my hands by my side and focused on my breathing. 5552. 5552. They came straight towards me, then brushed against me on both sides. I was the filling in a shark sandwich, but with my breath under control, I survived to tell the tale. The next time I felt nervous while waiting to go on stage for a speech, I gave myself a little pep talk – at least I didn't have to worry about being eaten alive that day!

STEP THREE – THE OVERRIDE SWITCH

Muhammad Ali is considered to be one of the greatest boxers and sportspeople of all time. He had a very powerful tool that helped him achieve a peak-performance mindset. He was known to predict openly the outcome of his fights before each event. He would visualise the fight over and over in his mind and then announce how he would beat his opponent before the event took place. He called this 'future history'. I've heard it said that he got so good at making his accurate predictions that gambling companies asked him to stop, because they couldn't take as many bets on his fights. He continued to visualise, but stopped broadcasting what he planned to do.

A few years ago, I was speaking at a conference and saw an excellent speaker deliver his session while I waited to go on. He described a terrific story about Ali. I have been unable to contact him since to verify my memory of this story, but wanted to share it with you in the way I remember him telling it.

He explained that his grandfather had worked with a charity and they managed to convince Ali to give them a pair of his boxing gloves to auction to raise money. Ali also gave them a couple of tickets to come along and watch a fight.

When the fifth round of the fight started, Ali came out swinging hard and knocked out his opponent with the first punch. The crowd cheered wildly and started rushing towards the ring. The grandfather thought he might get crushed, so he began backing away. Ali shouted to him and said, 'Take the gloves!' and threw them to him.

As he walked away, clutching the gloves tightly, the grandfather heard Ali shout to him again. 'Look in the gloves!' So the man looked. Inside one glove Ali had written in large white letters 'Fifth round' and in the other glove 'First punch'. That was Ali's future history.

Many other athletes are known to visualise their success, including Andy Murray, who became the first British man to win Wimbledon in seventy-seven years. Others include rugby player Jonny Wilkinson, who put part of his success down to imagining the exact way in which he would kick a ball during a match to help him score. British heptathlete Jessica Ennis Hill visualised her gold-winning Olympic events. British Olympic cyclist Chris Hoy visualised every detail of his 2012 gold-winning Olympic race hundreds of times, so that he was crystal clear in his mind on exactly what he was going to do and the result he would get. Even when the timing technology went wrong, he remembers feeling totally in control. When he crossed the finish line, he knew that he had achieved the fastest time, just as he had visualised.

Hoy's story doesn't finish there, though. At the end of the race, a strange feeling came over him. He hadn't visualised what would happen when he won, so he simply raised an arm up in the air to celebrate. He wondered if it was real – or part of his visualisation.

That is the power of this technique – if you visualise clearly enough then your mind won't know the difference between reality and your imagination. It will believe that you have succeeded at your event many times before, you will have overridden your monkey mind and you will be free to perform at your best.

PUTTING VISUALISATION INTO PRACTICE

Having suffered from a crippling fear of speaking to groups of people, I have used my own version of future history for many years. Over the course of a decade, I would go for a walk or run every day, Monday to Friday, first thing in the morning, to visualise my future. I would usually focus on an upcoming event and imagine it going brilliantly well. I still do it now when I need to.

I learned that the best technique was to focus on how I wanted to feel and the actions that I would take. We can't control technology; nor can we control other people. We can each control only what we do, think and feel. If your actions, thoughts and feelings are the subject of your visualisation, nothing can throw you off the path.

The first ever one-day workshop that I taught was a daunting prospect. I had no intention of running a workshop as long as that until people started asking for it. Then a film company got in touch and asked me to coach someone, the subject of their documentary, to improve his chances of success at interview. I booked a venue, then set to work thinking about what I should teach.

I want everyone who attends my workshops to leave feeling it was one of the best days of their career. I'm always delighted and humbled when we get this kind of feedback. But back then, the first time, I had no idea how it would turn out. I had to rely on visualisation to give my monkey mind confidence that everything would go well.

I worked hard for weeks to get the content ready. I would go for a walk or run every morning and visualise delivering a successful event.

On the morning of the workshop, as I drove to the venue, I remember playing the Queen song 'Under Pressure' in the car, just to make myself laugh and get in the zone for a good day.

Everything went perfectly, exactly as I'd imagined. There were some tough questions from the participants and film crew throughout the day, but I was able to manage my state without flinching. In the afternoon, one person raised his hand and said, 'How did you manage to become so good at this? You haven't said erm or umm the entire day!' I laughed. The visualisation had truly worked.

Shortly after this came another booking that was a huge deal for me. Medical opinion leaders from twenty-one countries were being gathered in Prague for a conference to discuss oncology treatments. They needed a team who could coach the doctors to become better communicators. They wanted a conference chairman, keynote speaker and a team of ten coaches to deliver breakout coaching to the one hundred people at the event.

We had never done any of this before. I had done only jobs in the UK either by myself or with one other person. And we had coached a maximum of twenty people at a time. I had no idea how to be a chairman, or who would be on my team. Plus, the one person I usually had alongside me was unavailable for the dates!

I hustled hard for months to put everything together until I knew we were ready to provide a terrific experience. I still remember very clearly the feeling of walking up on stage at the start of the conference.

It was my first time speaking to such a prestigious audience. As I turned to look at them all, I felt as if a needle had penetrated my chest and directly injected my heart with adrenaline. I tried to speak and stuttered the first few words. I stopped. This was it – make-or-break time. If I succeeded at this event, it could lead to many more bookings and a much larger, international business. If I failed I would be letting down the experts in the room, my team and the client who had believed in me.

At the back of the long conference room I noticed the client, sitting hunched over, his hands in the prayer position, as if thinking, 'Please be good!'

I took a slow breath and closed my eyes. To my amazement, during that long blink I saw the event in my mind going exactly as I had visualised it. I saw myself speaking passionately, moving confidently and feeling in control. I opened my eyes and the oxygen filled my lungs. I began to speak with new energy. We were off.

By the end of the conference, the feedback we were getting was so positive that we worked with that client for more than a decade, at events all around the world. On the way home from that first event, sitting in Prague airport, I cried tears of sheer joy.

YOUR FUTURE HISTORY IN TEN STEPS

For best results I recommend you do this ten-step activity while walking, which allows you to loosen up your body, breathe deeply and fill your body with feel-good hormones. Your mind will associate these positive feelings with your future event. If sitting or standing is a better option for you, though, that's fine too. Just make sure you're upright, with your feet flat on the floor, so that you have an uplifted posture. If you're walking look ahead or up, don't hunch and look at the ground. You can listen to music too, if you want to. Here are the ten steps.

1) Take a few slow, deep breaths to calm your mind (the 5552 method will work well here, if you're standing or sitting still).

2) Think about your past peak-state experiences. Remember them as vividly as you can, enjoying the feeling of what happened when you were at your best. Keep filling your mind with as many peak experiences as you can. Take your time to enjoy them fully.

3) Next, focus on your core values – what are the three areas that you care about most in life, the principles that you live by, the things that define your best self?

4) Think about a future event that is making you feel anxious.

5) Imagine the event as clearly as you can, including the location and people who will be there.

6) See the event unfold, from the start of the day onwards. Imagine feeling in a peak state as you do all of the necessary things to ensure success. (Keep the focus on what you're thinking, doing, feeling, not on what else might or might not go on around you.)

7) As you go through the event moment by moment in fine detail, feel the peak state in your mind and body – the state you would like to be in on the day.

8) Then imagine celebrating after the event, having done everything you needed in order to perform at your best.

9) Think backwards from the event to the present day and consider this – what do you need to do between now and then in order for everything to go well? How can you prepare? How often will you visualise?

10) Write down those preparation steps and start working on them from today. Your monkey will feel at ease knowing that you're taking care of him.

Repeat this as often as you need to. At first I would visualise my future history every day, at the start of the day, in order to get the routine in my mind, settle any fears and start my day positively.

If there's one activity or piece of advice you take away from this book, I hope it is this ten-step strategy. I have found that many people know what they need to do in order to succeed, but they simply aren't doing it. Why? Mindset. They don't believe they can do it. Their monkey mind prevents them from behaving in a way that will let them succeed, for fear of failure. By working on your mindset daily, you can change that identity and belief, move towards your goals and achieve the success you really deserve.

Even if you think you don't need to practise the strategy, or already do something similar, I implore you to try it this way for two weeks. Two consistent weeks of focussing on a future event for fifteen minutes per day (longer if you can – I used to do forty-five minutes per day, including a walk and listening to music), following those ten steps, I'm sure will be enough to show you results.

Will you commit to doing this? I'm not going to write anything else until you say yes, so... okay, you're in!

Great. Do it. Then email me and tell me what happened. I'd love to hear from you, because I know how much this has helped me and transformed the personal and professional lives of the people I have been teaching for decades. Enjoy!

AND FINALLY... CELEBRATE

There is one element in that ten-step process that we need to look at in a bit more detail – celebration.

For many years I would just achieve a goal, get terrific feedback and move on to the next event. Then I noticed my personal motivation levels going downwards, as if my monkey mind was saying 'Again?! You want me to go through another huge event that requires weeks of preparation, visualising and reaching the limits of your potential again?! Why?! What do I get out of this?'

For a long time the act of doing the event, feeling proud of myself and fulfilled by the work I was doing was enough to keep driving me forwards, but eventually I felt worn down. I hired a business coach who reminded me of the importance of celebration. She told me about the actor Sir Anthony Hopkins, who had spoken about the need to celebrate to remain motivated. He had realised he was losing his love of acting because he just kept working and never celebrated his achievements, even his Academy Award.

The propsect of celebration hard-wires the mind for success. If your monkey mind knows that there is a reward at the other side of a tough event, it's more willing to stay in line when you need it to.

One note of caution, though. Material rewards won't necessarily fulfil you. In one talk, journalist and best-selling author Daniel Pink spoke about 'the puzzle of motivation'. He explained that you can motivate people to do a simple task with small rewards, but complex tasks require something more. People need to feel inherently fulfilled by the experience in order to keep pushing past challenges and driving themselves beyond the point at which others would stop.

Motivational speaker Simon Sinek also mentioned this in his book, *Start With Why*. He explained that in the early 1900s, Samuel Pierpont Langley set out to create the first successful aeroplane. He had a $50,000 grant from the War Department and the greatest minds and materials gathered around him. Meanwhile, the Wright Brothers were also trying to build a plane, but they had no grant, no higher education and worked on their plans in a bicycle shop. Despite their lack of resources, they succeeded first. Why? Because they had rallied and inspired everyone around them to achieve greatness through doing work that would make them proud.

So, if you're considering motivating yourself or your team by buying a fancy watch or giving them a bonus, lovely – but it will go only so far. Internal enjoyment of the achievement and a sense of fulfilment are far more important. If you want to achieve big and complex goals, you must ensure that you care deeply about the underlying reason why you're pursuing them.

When you have reached the goal, how will you celebrate? After you complete an important event, you may want to share the journey you experienced with someone who cares about you. This will help you to feel connected to them, give greater meaning to the accomplishment and give you both a sense of pride.

Then you might want to treat yourself to something fun, to blow off steam before you climb the next mountain. When choosing a way to celebrate, I also advise that you don't include unhealthy food, recreational drugs, or alcohol as the focus of your celebrations. Think instead about indulging in something that won't harm you.

Have a think now – what would be a wonderful celebration for you after you succeed at your next important event? Make it something you genuinely feel excited about.

Viva Las Vegas!

One of my regular clients asked me to speak to 1,000 people on their sales team at an event in Las Vegas. I had already trained their European sales team and my contact in Europe had told her colleagues in the US that I was amazing. They had high expectations.

A month before the event, I called the organisers to discuss the details. All seemed well until they shared with me a floor plan of 1,000 people sitting at rows of tables on a flat floor space. This meant that people would be a very long way from me and spread out from each other. I've always preferred having people as close to me as possible, so that they can see my face clearly. It also helps to have people sitting closer to each other: enjoyment, like laughter, is infectious.

More importantly I was intending to write notes on a flipchart for people, as I explored deeper strategies with them. How would they be able to see what I was writing and follow the session?

I asked if the organisers could change the layout. They said no. The fire department of Las Vegas has strict policies on room layouts and has to approve every event. The layout had already been approved and we were not allowed to change it. I asked if they were going to film the event, so that people could see my face on the big screen and feel connected to me. Nope. So I asked if it was possible for me to write some strategies on a flipchart or screen that everyone would be able to see. Ah! There would be a special smart board that would magically transmit everything I wrote up onto the screen and that way everyone in the room would easily see it.

I didn't feel good about this. My monkey started jabbering, 'It will fail. You'll look like an idiot. One thousand people will laugh at you and boo you off stage. Abort the mission now!'

I began applying the ten-step mindset strategy to the event. I practised about three times per week as I went running. I pictured myself in a peak state and visualised people feeling connected to me. I decided that on the day of the event, I would arrive ninety minutes before anyone else, in order to check the fancy equipment. That way I would calm my monkey and feel ready to do my best work.

I spoke to the technicians a week before the event, agreed the plan and everything was set. I even checked my route to the venue the day before, so that I knew exactly where I was going. At 7am I arrived at the meeting room and strode in confidently to get things ready.

I asked where the head technician was. 'He's sick today.' Ah. I asked where the magical smart board was. 'Oh,' they said. 'It's probably in a store room somewhere and we've never used it before. Besides, we can't even get the projector screens to work.' Yikes.

My monkey mind went from happily snoozing to fully alert.

It took a full hour for them to simply plug in my laptop, which is usually a thirty-second job. Then the sound didn't work. After another ten minutes, they figured out the problem. Meanwhile an assistant had pulled a dusty old white board out of a cupboard and was attempting to attach smart-board magnets to it. He looked sweaty, flustered and confused. 'I have no idea how this works,' he said.

With ten minutes left until the audience walked in, I asked him to keep trying, while his colleague found me a microphone.

Five minutes to go. The roar of the audience outside the doors was building. They were all enjoying breakfast in the hallway, while we scrabbled around trying to get the technology to work. My monkey was setting off grenades in my brain. It was time to hit the override switch. I turned to the team, smiled and said, 'Let's put the smart board away. Turn on the music. Open the doors.'

I walked calmly to sit at the side of the room as 1,000 people dashed in, rushing to get a good seat, looking forward to the morning's event. I sat in an uplifted position, took deep breaths using the 5552 rhythm to lower my heart rate and dissipate the stress hormones. I thought about past events where I had overcome challenges and I recalled my core values. Then I reflected on the visualisations I had done for this event. I had even gone running up and down the Las Vegas strip the day before. I told my monkey mind, 'I feel excited. I'm in the right place. I know what I'm doing.' He replied 'You do?! Let me check – yes, you're right! Thank goodness! Okay, you're the boss.'

As I walked to the stage, I felt an extraordinary state of ease. I was far more at ease than I would normally expect. I spoke with full confidence and enthusiasm. As I reached the moment where I needed the smart board, I flipped into Plan B (there's always a Plan B because I never rely on technology). I explained everything and kept the room engaged without needing the smart board. I could even see the tiny dots of people at the back busily writing notes. We finished the event with loud applause and happy faces.

As people were leaving, the company's training team came up to greet me on the stage. They wanted to take a photo with me. To me this was the greatest honour and a humbling way to be thanked. As a fellow teacher I felt blessed to gain their praise.

As I left, the venue my monkey said, 'Pheweeee!!!! That was exhausting, but we did it... so how are we going to celebrate?!'

I know what you may be thinking. It's Vegas. Surely that meant a night of gambling, drinking and dancing on tables? Not for me. Negative rewards can cause a toxic tail-spin that destroys your health, career and the people around you. That's why it's important to celebrate in a positive, empowering way that genuinely fulfils you.

First, I rang my family to share the success of the event with them. They laughed and cheered at everything I had lived through. Then I booked a treat. The next morning, at the crack of dawn, I took a flight to the Grand Canyon. I got in a helicopter and sat next to the pilot. We flew out to enjoy the magnificent beauty below. The pilot glanced at my smiling face as we got close to the edge. He switched songs on his iPod and played the theme music from the movie *Top Gun* as the epic view unfolded beneath us. I grinned so much that my cheeks hurt. My monkey mind felt grateful. I still think back to this amazing experience when I have other big events coming up, recalling the challenges, the pressure I felt, the positive state I maintained, the fulfilment of doing my best work for people and the celebration afterwards.

Since then, my monkey mind has felt more at ease about all kinds of events, thinking, 'Don't worry, it will all be worth it.'

So what will your celebration be?

First, focus on intrinsic value – what will you achieve simply by working towards an upcoming challenge or event? It's important to feel that the journey will be worthwhile no matter what happens, even if you don't win the pitch or get the job. What learning will you take away? How will this help you grow your skills? Being fulfilled regardless of the outcome will ensure your monkey mind won't resist taking on the next challenge.

Second, who will you connect with afterwards to share the story? I've found that the conversations I have with friends and family after big events are so important. Opening up about what happened will amplify any feelings of pride or fulfilment; or it gives your loved ones an opportunity to be compassionate and console you, if things didn't go so well.

Third, what will you do for yourself as a positive reward? It needn't be expensive. Sometimes, putting on some music and dancing around screaming 'Yes!' is enough to feel good. Muttering yes under your breath isn't enough, though. Your monkey will end up saying, 'Is that it?!?!' You need to celebrate the way that children do it.

Born to celebrate

One of our natural instincts for celebration is to raise our hands above our head. This is true across different cultures, and even for people who are born blind. It is an instinctive demonstration of victory.

Jumping up and down releases endorphins, feel-good hormones. That's why athletes do it; and why children across the globe do it when they hear they'll be having pancakes for breakfast. (Or, perhaps that's just my house.) So here's a celebration that will feel great and keep you motivated and won't cost you a penny:

- Think of your favourite high-energy music.
- Crank it up loudly the next time you achieve a goal.
- Jump up and down with your arms above your head, and dance like no one's watching.
- Shout 'Yes!'
- Keep going for thirty seconds.

Finally, it's important not to revel too long in your success. Take time to enjoy the moment. Connect with people. Say kind words to yourself. Then set the next goal. By doing so you'll be in the best state possible to succeed when you experience the inevitable obstacles and objections that a new goal may throw in your way.

Chapter 12
You were born to collaborate

Four out of ten. The worst feedback I've ever been given. It was the day I nearly quit. Despite everything I knew about style, story and state, it had all fallen apart because I'd forgotten one simple thing.

No matter how brilliant your delivery, content and mindset are, people will still disagree with you, interrupt you and object. How you handle these objections can make or break your success.

Learning how to handle objections is the final hurdle to communicating as you were born to do it. It requires a shift in your mindset. You'll need to move away from the mental and emotional state you're most likely to approach difficult situations in towards a braver path – the path that all of us need to take if we are to succeed. You need to use the greatest strength we are born with – collaboration.

Many of our clients feel that they're already good at collaboration. They assure me that they listen well, have empathy and reach positive resolutions whenever they're challenged. However, when they step up to the front of the room and are given a practice objection, they usually get flustered or defensive. It is not as easy as it first seems.

I also used to feel I was good at handling objections, until one event revealed my weakness. About ten years ago, I agreed to run a workshop for an electronics company. I pitched to their decision makers and they booked me to train their executive team.

I prepared myself thoroughly, researched who I was working with and understood their challenges and goals. I worked on my content, delivery and mindset and felt ready to give them my best.

At the start of the workshop, I explained how people will ignore even the greatest ideas if the person communicating the ideas does so badly. 'For example,' I said, 'people keep saying, "this is the greatest idea since sliced bread", but even sliced bread was a failed concept at first. People didn't want to listen, until the Wonder company came along to improve the marketing. When the sliced-bread makers communicated the value of the idea, it became a huge success. I want to make sure that people hear your ideas and act on them.'

At this point a woman who was sitting at the back of the room shouted out, 'Our ideas aren't good. They're boring. They're dull. They're not sliced bread. This isn't relevant to us.' I wasn't expecting her objection, but I tried to address her point: 'Well, that's okay. Don't worry if you feel that your ideas are dull or complex, I'll share with you ways you can communicate them in a more engaging way.'

I thought I had dealt with her comment fairly well. The woman sat quietly… until the next day when a tirade of negativity unfolded. Whenever I asked the group to do an activity, they all did it willingly, apart from her. At every turn she insisted that the strategies were useless, the coaching was pointless and that there was no way that anyone could possibly follow what I was asking them to do. Other people rolled their eyes at her. She kept muttering, 'What a waste of time!' continually sighing and refusing to take part.

At the end of the event, on her feedback sheet she gave me a score of four out of ten. Everyone else gave a nine or ten. Normally, I'm crushed if I get a nine! After every event, I review the feedback and if there is anything less than a ten in any area, I look at ways to make sure it's a ten next time. Her behaviour and her score made me feel like giving up teaching. I had failed her, failed myself and let down the rest of the group. Where had I gone wrong?

You may be thinking, 'Don't worry, Richard, all the other people liked it, you can't please everyone.' There was a large part of my brain yelling this at me, insisting I was great and it was her fault if she couldn't see it. After all, many thousands of people had enjoyed my workshops before her. Other people who attended that same event thought it was great. Why bother worrying about her reaction?

I needed to learn from it. The question that has driven me forwards since I began teaching is how could I do it better? At the end of a different two-day event to improve the training skills of eight professional trainers, every one of them spontaneously stood up to give us a standing ovation. I said to my colleagues 'So how do we improve on this tomorrow? What could we do better?' They thought I was joking. 'What more do you want? They absolutely loved it!' But we should always strive to improve.

That's why I couldn't shake the experience at the electronics company. I kept going back over the event, thinking, 'What could I have done differently? If that happens again, what could I do?'

I thought about what the woman had really meant when she first spoke up. Effectively, she'd said, 'You don't understand my problems.' I acknowledged her comment, but I moved on too quickly. I had missed an opportunity to hear her voice, connect with her and help her to feel understood.

As frustrated as you may feel when people object, interrupt or say something negative, I encourage you to pause. Aim to connect with them and hear more of their voice, rather than less. In this way you may discover insights that weren't previously clear to you. Some of those insights may be critical to your ability to communicate effectively with everyone in the room.

TELL ME MORE

Any event or pitch will break down if not everyone in the room buys into the same story. When there are two opposing views, people stop collaborating. If people disagree with you, then you must take the time to understand how they see the world, so that you can find agreement and move forwards together.

I'd failed to do this with the negative woman. I felt that I knew her situation well enough through my weeks of preparation and research. I thought that my story and expertise would be convincing enough to win her around. Looking back, I believe she felt that I hadn't heard her voice, or understood her view of the world, so not only did she stop listening, she did everything she could to disrupt the event from that point forwards.

What if I'd stopped? What if I'd shown genuine concern and said, 'Tell me more. I'm here to help and we can tailor the workshop to give you what you need. Can you describe the challenges you face?' What if I'd then stopped to truly listen to her answers? She would have felt heard and valued. That would have been a huge step forwards.

Before we look at exactly how to best handle an objection, let's think about what most people do when someone listening to them throws a challenge at them.

The objection-handling system

In 2009 my team went to work in Orlando, Florida, at one of the Disney World hotels. We were there to coach a delegation of salespeople on how to handle challenging conversations.

Before the event started, one of their leaders told me that he didn't want us to teach our method for dealing with objections, because his company already had one. He acknowledged that it wasn't working, but he didn't want us to change it, he wanted us to coach the sales team on how to use their own system better.

As soon as he showed me the system, it was obvious to me why it didn't work. This is it:

Acknowledge $\longrightarrow$ Verify $\longrightarrow$ Respond $\longrightarrow$ Close

Can you notice what's missing? Think about what mindset this system suggests, compared with the best state we need to be in to handle objections. I tried to explain that he needed to change the system. He told me that their system was based on research. They had put it on the company intranet and printed it in every copy of the manual that every member of the sales team would receive at the conference. I asked him why he felt it wasn't working. He told me, 'It feels clunky, our clients don't respond well to it, our team members are a bit wooden when they use it. Maybe you could show them how to be less robotic?' It's not unusual for companies to try to polish up something they've developed to save it from failure, but sometimes you just need to admit that the problem isn't the delivery. Sometimes, the problem is the system itself. They say only a bad workman blames his tools, but if you're trying to hit a nail into the wall with a sponge, you won't get very far.

I tried a different approach. I explained that the system was robotic, not the people using it. He didn't understand, so I asked if this leader had any children or pets. He had one daughter, aged five, and a hamster. 'Okay,' I said. 'Hamsters don't live very long, so that means that someday soon you'll come home from work and your daughter will come up to you with tears in her eyes and say, "Daddy, my hamster just died." Now imagine that you use your robotic system to handle that situation. Perhaps you say, "I **acknowledge** the hamster is dead. Let me just **verify** it (shake, shake, sniff, sniff), yep the hamster is dead. My **response** is that we get a new one. That's the end of the conversation!' You're not going to win parent of the year with that approach.' He laughed. I'd got through to him.

Children show their emotions freely. As adults we tend to keep them inside more, but we still have them. So what was the main problem with their system? Have you guessed it? There's no emotion in it. It sounds like a computer process. It's highly logical.

People like logic, though, of course. And many people will push back when I tell them that logic alone is a problem. There's nothing wrong with being logical, but remember that your brain is built to respond emotionally first and logically second. The emotional part of your brain is running the show. Objections are emotional. If you want to connect with a person, you have to connect with their emotions first.

The clue is often in the words people use and their tone of voice. Have you noticed how many objections start with people saying, 'I just really feel that…' or 'There is no way this will work, nobody will agree to it.' You can sense the emotion. You can even hear the emotion in seemingly logical sentences, just by listening to the tone: 'Have you seen the profit margin for the last quarter?' This could be a straightforward question, but if the tone sounds sceptical, incredulous or frustrated, then this question is actually masking an objection. It might mean, for example, 'We can't afford what you're suggesting.'

No matter what the objection, though, Acknowledge $\longrightarrow$ Verify $\longrightarrow$ Respond $\longrightarrow$ Close is likely to make matters worse, not better.

So, how do we approach challenging moments, objections or conversations, in a way that leads to the best end result for you and the person with the challenge?

Imagine a friend of yours was feeling really worried about something. What would you need to do to help them to feel comfortable enough to open up and tell you about their problem? You would need to show them that you care, you would need to empathise. Sensing your empathy, your friend's monkey mind would relax and your friend would open up to you. Then, you would be able to collaborate to find a solution. You'd become a team – and that's how human beings have survived for thousands of years.

EMPATHISE

Let me give you an example of how empathy can diffuse the bomb. When the world first gave us Internet banking, I thought it would be a wonderful way to save time in my business, so I contacted our bank and asked how it worked. They said I had to fill out a twelve-page form, which they would send me in the post.

'Can't I do this online?!' I asked, feeling confused.

'No,' they told me. 'For legal reasons you have to fill this out on paper and sign it.' Even now, this seems utterly bizarre. In years to come, people may read this and wonder how on earth banks existed with such archaic ways of working. But the paper form was what they needed, so they sent me one.

I filled out the form, all twelve pages, then sent it back. I didn't hear anything for a month, so I gave them a call.

'Hello, I sent my form to you, are we now online?' I asked.

They accessed my details and said, 'Ah, no, we haven't created your online account because you left two questions blank on your form.' Hmm. I asked the call handler if she had my paper form in front of her, which she did. I offered to give her the answers to the two questions, so that she could fill them out for me. Nope, not possible, legal reasons...

'Okay then, can you post back my original form so that I can get it done?' Of course she could. But what did I get in the post the following week? That's right – a new form. I filled it out, checked every box, sent it back and again heard nothing. I phoned them and said, 'Are we now online?'

No, they told me, they had never received my form. It turned out that there had been a problem with their post, a bunch of letters went missing. They offered to send me another form.

'Can't we just do this online?!' I asked again. No, for legal reasons another form would be posted to me. When the third form arrived I had no interest in filling it out. Internet banking was supposed to be efficient and it was wasting my time and energy and testing my patience. I left the form on my desk for several months until I finally relented. I filled it out, checked every box and then posted it by recorded delivery. The following day I got a call from the bank.

'Hello Mr Newman, we have your form here.'

'Terrific!' I cried. 'Does that mean we are now online?!'

'Well, no.' Steam started coming out of my ears. 'I'm not sure how long you've had this form for, but we had a lot of complaints about how long it was, so we've created a shorter form and I'll send you a copy today.' My head exploded. My patience had gone. I should have stayed calm. I didn't. I let out months of agitation on the poor lady sitting at the end of the phone.

'Another form!! I have wasted nearly six months trying to get online with you! I've filled in countless forms! First, the form wasn't good enough. Then, you lost the form! Now, you've changed the form!? That's it. We're taking all of our money and we're going to give it to your competitor. How do you feel about that?' What reaction do you expect I received? I think the most likely reactions would be:

- To put the phone down.

- To say, 'If you could please calm down, sir...'

- To say, 'Well, that's not my fault. We are just following our procedure.'

- To follow the Orlando company's system and say, 'I

acknowledge what you said, I can verify it's true, my response is that I'm sending you another form, goodbye." (If she'd done that, I would have screamed.)

She did none of these. Here's what she actually said:

'Six months? Oh no, I can't believe it! It's no wonder you're feeling frustrated. I imagine I would feel exactly the same in your position. In fact, I'm going to report this to my manager so that this doesn't happen to anyone else.' I was stunned. She empathised. The frustration disappeared.

'Oh, that's okay, don't worry,' I said, suddenly feeling calm. 'I'm sure we can work this out.'

She sent me a form. We got online. We're still with that bank today. Why? Because she heard me. She connected. She spoke to me the way that a human is supposed to talk to another human.

You may be thinking, 'Great, empathy, yes, I can do that. I'm a decent person. I probably empathise all the time.' But you may feel differently when you pitch an idea that you care about. When people start objecting, empathy can quickly disappear. Instead, we try to convince our objectors that we are right and they are wrong.

Empathy is easy when you agree with people. It's much harder when you're in front of a room of twenty decision makers, saying, 'It's blue, it's blue, it's blue', and one of them says, 'No it's not blue, it's red.' The public rejection of an idea you care about hurts. You have to stay calm. You have to listen. You have to empathise. If you don't, your idea can die in the cross-fire. Empathy is about seeing life through someone else's eyes, walking in their shoes, showing you care.

ACTION!

When someone objects you must forget about your slides, ignore your script, switch off your agenda and listen.

Some people say that they don't have time to nurture objectors through their interruption, because when there are only twenty minutes to talk, they have to finish their content. You can email your content. You can't handle objections by email. You must handle objections while you're in the room, because that's the best way to show you understand. Once your audience feels heard and understood, you're far more likely to gain their commitment.

Empathise like you mean it. See the world through your objector's eyes and let them talk while you aim to understand where their pain comes from. Then...

CLARIFY

Imagine walking into a doctor's office with a pain in your leg. After the doctor empathises for a few moments, he or she says, 'Okay let's chop it off then!' You would hop out of their office as fast as your good leg could carry you!

People do this in business all the time. They pretend to empathise, but they never listen long enough to find out what the real problem is. Instead, they jump into solution mode. Try to resist this urge to fix things quickly. After you've listened and empathised, you need to clarify, in order to fully understand what the person needs from you.

Think back to the storytelling chapter – people are driven by pain and pleasure. If you're going to reach an agreement with someone in a meeting, pitch or negotiation, you need to know what is driving their behaviour. What pain do they want to avoid? What does a better future look like for them?

A doctor will ask you questions like this:

- Can you tell me more about the problem you're experiencing?

- Can you explain how it started?

- Can you describe the pain?

These questions are TED questions (Tell, Explain, Describe). They are designed to get you to open up and share more specific information, so that the doctor gains a clearer picture of the problem. It also gives the doctor some thinking time.

Can you remember how you felt after the last objection or disagreement you had to deal with? Many of us wrestle with that moment for days afterwards, wondering what we could have done differently. A few days later you may think, 'That's what I should have said!' You feel delighted to have realised where you went wrong, but then deflated, wishing you had thought of it at the time. What if you could gain this extra thinking time in the moment? You can. But not if you start talking! You must stop and listen.

Ask open questions, so that the person objecting talks for 80 percent of the time. Just nudge the person along, as you investigate the heart of the issue together. You may feel like rushing in with an answer, so that you can be the all-knowing expert, but don't. A solution may genuinely appear to you as your objector starts talking, but keep it to yourself. Think WAIT – Why Am I Talking? If you're talking you can't be listening, understanding or thinking about a helpful response. Your instant idea of a solution is most likely to crash and burn. It's too soon. You don't know what the person wants yet. Just like storytelling, you need to establish the source of the pain, so that you can work towards the pleasure. Help yourself and your objector: pause to listen. Then ask questions that reveal the truth of the problem – they are gold dust for overcoming challenges and collaborating on solutions. For example:

- What would you like to achieve today?

- What's the most important area for you?

Don't shy away from asking more questions to find out what your objector really needs, even when you're speaking to a large group. Some speakers will rush their response when there are lots of people watching them because they feel stressed – but rushing just risks your credibility. Whether the group is large or small, if you don't clarify the issue before announcing your solution, the person who asked the question just feels dismayed, because your solution doesn't help him or her achieve a desired better future. How could it? You didn't find out what your objector really needed. In a large group, the person is left deflated – and that feeling just ripples throughout the room. Think of it this way: most objections are like the tip of the iceberg – you need to delve beneath to find the extent of the problem, whether that's with one person watching or 1,000 eager people, all eyes fixed on you. Handling a challenge well gives others confidence in you – the other people in the room will see it as a true strength.

How would it be if somebody interrupted you and said, 'Your idea will never work because my team is already overwhelmed with other projects.' Rather than ripping up your idea and accepting defeat, you could do the following:

- **Empathise**: 'Thanks for raising that issue. I agree it's important that people don't feel overwhelmed.'
- **Clarify pain**: 'Can you tell me more about the challenges you feel we may face? Could you explain what the main problem may be from your perspective?'
- **Clarify pleasure**: 'We have to resolve this issue before the end of the year, so could you describe what the ideal solution would look like for you?'

By doing this, in a real, human, empathetic way, you're allowing the person to talk about issues that they care about, you get to understand any obstacles that may get in the way of moving forward and you learn what the better future looks like – from their perspective. At that point you're in a state of collaboration. You're able to work out a solution that will work for everyone.

Often, a solution will come down to timing. The team is too busy in October, so you'll need to intervene with your plan in November, for example. You still get to complete your project before the end of the year and the people involved feel that you care.

There won't always be neat solutions like this, of course. Sometimes you'll get people with objections that you cannot resolve, but it is still important to show that you care and to listen. That way everyone in the room will know that you are there to help, rather than to shout about your great idea.

I once attended a conference that was about health and nutrition. I had been told that the speaker was terrific and I should really see him in action, so I did – along with thousands of other people. And he was great. He had us all listening intently throughout the morning. We were all thinking carefully about what we ate at lunchtime and talking about how good he was as a speaker.

Part way through the afternoon he said, 'We have some extra time, does anyone have any questions?' Lots of hands went up. He rushed to welcome the first question, pointing to a lady who was sitting near to me. She stood up and said, 'I came on this seminar last year. I've been doing everything you said and I feel terrible. My friends tell me I smell. I can't sleep. What should I do?'

The room hushed. His face was being filmed and projected onto the big screens around him. He looked like a rabbit stuck in the headlights. We had all been totally convinced by his teaching up to that point, but now we were worried that we would end up feeling like this lady if we followed his advice. In order to reassure the whole audience and help her, he needed to show compassion, understand what the cause of the problem might be and find a solution for her.

If he had investigated what the real issue was he could have revealed another amazing nugget for everyone else to remember, made her feel relieved and danced off stage as a hero. He didn't. He rushed it. Worse still, he dismissed her without a moment of empathy, even though she had followed his teachings and evidently paid to attend two of his seminars. 'Err, drink twice as much water!' he said, before walking to the other side of the stage and saying, 'Who has another question over here?'

He lost the room. She remained standing, saying, 'What?! Is that it? He doesn't care. He doesn't know what he's doing.' The rest of the room felt unsettled and he went from hero to zero in an instant.

Perhaps his answer was correct, but we would never know. He responded to her cry for help with a shotgun approach. Aiming to rapidly fire a quick response in her direction and move on might have seemed expedient, but she needed more than an answer. She needed empathy, understanding, investigation and collaboration on an agreed way forward.

Is the objection relevant?

You may come across objections that don't seem relevant to anyone else in the room. As always, whatever happens, don't rush it. Don't be too quick to dismiss the objector, but do check if the conversation is of value for everyone else. Ask the other people in the room if they're also experiencing the problem. If it's relevant to just one person out of fifty, then you can agree to discuss it afterwards. If other people are having the same issue, put your agenda aside and listen, then resolve things together. When people feel they have contributed to a solution, they feel more committed to it.

So, once you've taken your time, shown warmth, shown humanity, connected and understood, you need to...

PROPOSE

At this point in the objection cycle, you may be feeling fairly confident that you have a solution. You may be tempted to say, 'I know what to do! This will fix everything!' The common fate of this approach is that you put forward what you feel is a brilliant idea and it gets shot down. Then it feels as if the whole process has been a waste of time and you'll feel too dejected to try again.

Let's look at a different way forward. Think about getting engaged. If you love someone and things are moving in the right direction, you might perhaps book a fancy dinner in a romantic location, order Champagne, get down on bended knee and say, 'You will marry me!' Nope. Not gonna work. All the Champagne and nice food in the world won't help you pull that one off. Even a person who was feeling ready and willing to walk side by side with you for ever would feel annoyed if you said that. The same is true in business.

If you're moving forward well in a challenging conversation, remember that it's not your job to fix everything, create a big solution and answer every problem. You just need to collaborate. Rather than telling someone else what to do next, try proposing.

'Will you marry me?' works so well because it implies free will. The person has a choice. In business you can achieve the same thing by saying, 'So if...'. For example, you might say, 'So if you had delivery by Christmas, would that work for you?' Propose your idea in the form of a question.

If your idea meets resistance, you haven't lost anything. You haven't put this suggestion forward as your one and only solution. You're still investigating options. You may need to empathise and clarify some more, but you're still part of the discussion that will enable you to reach a solution that works. If they like your suggestion, though, you're almost done.

CHECK

In order to be sure that you have covered everything in the objection, you must always check in before you move on. The last thing you want is any lingering uncertainty that may fester and raise further objections to your ideas later. Better to get it all dealt with straightaway. Everyone in the room will respect you for your ability to stay with the issue to a full resolution.

You can check in by saying:

- Does that answer your question?

- Does that give you everything you need?

- Was that helpful for you?

If the answer to any of those questions is no, then you can clarify further and work together to reach a resolution.

Of course, no process is going to resolve absolutely everything, but if you follow the advice in this chapter, you'll begin your event in the spirit (and state) of collaboration. And that will give you the best chance of a positive result.

A FEW EXTRA THOUGHTS...

Just before we move on, here are a few more pointers to keep in mind when you deal with objections:

- **Don't pretend to have empathy!** This is not a manipulation strategy to close more sales. It's about being human and treating people with respect. People will sense if you're just using a technique on them. Real empathy will serve you well.

- **Don't say 'but'**: if you say, 'I empathise with you, but...' you have just negated the empathy. And no, you can't simply swap 'But' for 'However'! Don't switch words, switch mindset.

- **Always ask yourself 'Why am I talking?'** Let the other person talk, so that you can listen, think, understand and help them best.

- **Collaborate.** Let people know that you care, understand the issues and then find a solution that works well for everyone.

Learning to master how to handle objections is perhaps the toughest part of being a speaker. But if you can do it well, your audience will view you as a true master of communication. Why? Because you will seem more human. They will see you can connect with people in the way you were born to do it.

FINAL THOUGHTS

BECOME THE PERSON
YOU WERE BORN TO BE

You have everything you need now. The principles, the proof and the process that will bring you back to how you were born to speak. So what's stopping you? There is one final challenge. Our need to fit in.

Brené Brown is well known for her research that shows that the opposite of belonging is not, in fact, being lonely. It's fitting in. Belonging means that no matter what we do, people will care about us and accept us. When we feel that people won't accept us for who we really are, we can lose ourselves by focusing on fitting in.

When you ignore the voice in your head that says, 'This is who I am, this is what I believe,' and just copy others, you're betraying yourself. Fitting in often means holding yourself back in order to be like people who are also probably just trying to fit in.

If you free yourself and stay true to who you were born to be, then you will inspire others to follow. This takes courage, but I believe it is the only way for you to feel fully alive.

During one of the lowest moments of my life, when I considered suicide, my struggle to fit in was fuelling my negative state of mind. What I really needed was a sense of belonging. At acting school I tried to apply everything we were learning, yet got continuous criticism from the tutors. I learned some wonderful skills from them, but trying to fit in with their expectations extinguished my joy of acting.

Women showed little interest in me, apart from one girl whom I started dating. She happened to comment that if I shaved my beard and cut my long hair, she wouldn't want to be with me anymore. She wanted me to fit in with her needs.

As I searched for a place to live in London, landlords and flatshares rejected me over and over, for months on end, despite my doing my best to be liked and fit in with what they were looking for. My dream life of moving to the city and building a life for myself felt in tatters.

As I travelled home each day, feeling that I didn't fit in with anyone around me, I would stand at the train station and think about jumping. I watched the trains arrive, wondering if I would die if I was hit by one of them. Then a friend recognised my pain and I opened up. After that I decided to live fully. I'd had enough of trying to fit in. It was causing too much pain. I just had to be me.

It was the fifth term of acting school. One of my teachers called this the '$%#& It Term'. He had noticed over the years that this was when students got sick of intellectual acting strategies and trusted their instincts. The good advice they had been given about stagecraft stayed with them and their bad habits were gone. They were ready to spread their wings and so they flew.

I was given a role called Osip in a Russian play. I gave it all I had, emotionally, physically and mentally. The day after a performance, every tutor at the school gave us lengthy critiques. But this time, I didn't want feedback. I took the day off.

The next day people rushed up to me and said, 'I can't believe you weren't here yesterday. Everybody loved your performance! They thought you had such presence! Even Alison!' Alison was a teacher who had been highly critical of me since I started studying there, because I didn't fit in with her beliefs about what an actor should be. She found me later that day, grabbed my hands and wouldn't let go. She looked into my eyes and said, 'Yes! You did it!' I was amazed.

I had broken free of my lifelong people-pleasing habit, doing what everyone around me seemed to expect of me, and I finally felt accepted. For the first time in six months of searching, I was offered a place to live. I turned it down. The person who lived there seemed very strict and I hadn't searched for that long only to stay with someone who made me feel uncomfortable. The next day I was offered another place with people I really liked. Living with them gave me some of the happiest days of my life.

That same year I was given the lead role in a youth production of *Fiddler on the Roof*. I followed my instincts and passionately expressed myself through the role. We gained a standing ovation from 1,000 people at every performance, which included my parents. They had been worried about me studying acting, but finally seemed confident that I had made the right choice.

On the final night of the show several lovely women in the cast gave me their phone numbers and asked me out on dates. What had happened? Why had everything changed?

I was still the same person, but I'd stripped away old habits, discovered how to express myself and trusted my inner voice. I stopped trying to fit in and became the real me. The version I was born to be. Speaking the way I was born to speak.

Twenty years later, as I walked off stage after an event, a lady came up to me and said 'I wish I could do that. You are clearly a natural.' You are too, I thought, you just don't know it yet.

As I reflected on my journey, through living with monks, studying acting, working with a Formula One team and teaching clients, I realised I had found my place. When I stand up to speak, aiming to help others, I know I am exactly where I belong. So are you.

So go ahead.

Breathe fully.

Put down your armour.

Stand up, speak out and be heard.

Become the person you were born to be.

Good luck with it all and let me know what happens next.

NOW – KEEP THE LEARNING GOING!

1) **Results -** Make sure your journey doesn't end here! Just go to **www.borntospeak.com/videos** now to get access to exclusive videos (if you haven't done so already).

2) **Review -** If you've enjoyed the book, will you please go to **www.amazon.co.uk** and leave a review? I'd really appreciate that.

3) **Recommend -** I want to help as many people as possible, so if you know someone who would benefit from reading this book, perhaps you can send them a copy.

Acknowledgements
Thank you

To my friends and family, you gave me support, laughter and a shoulder to lean on when I needed it, for which I will always be grateful.

To my team, thank you from the bottom of my heart for bringing the essence of this book alive every day, by delivering outstanding training events, with such passion, commitment and talent.

To our clients, it has been my honour to serve you, I feel humbled every time I see you step forward with courage. Put these ideas into action and gain the results you deserve.

And to those who helped turn my words into a book, you have enabled me to fulfil a dream, share the message and create something I will always be proud of.

Thank you all so much.